YOUR POWER TO CHANGE

YOUR POWER TO CHANGE

MASTER YOURSELF AND MASTER YOUR LIFE,
PAST, PRESENT, AND FUTURE.
THE POWER IS WITHIN YOU.

KYLE C. BECKER

YOUR POWER TO CHANGE
Copyright © 2023 by Kyle C. Becker

Copyright Registration Number TXU-2-266-189
All rights reserved under the Pan-American and International Copyright Conventions. This book may not be reproduced in whole or in part, except for brief quotations embodied in critical articles or reviews, in any form or by any means, electronic or mechanical, including photocopying, recording, or by any information storage and retrieval system now known or hereinafter invented, without written permission of the author.

PAPERBACK ISBN # – 978-17374732-0-6
HARDCOVER ISBN # – 978-17374732-2-0
ELECTRONIC ISBN # – 978-1-7374732-1-3

Any names, characters, and places featured in this publication are the result of the author's imagination. Any resemblance to actual persons (living or dead), places, events, circumstances, institutions, or anything else is purely incidental.

Publisher's Cataloging-In-Publication Data
(Prepared by The Donohue Group, Inc.)
Names: Becker, Kyle C., author
Title: Your Power to Change : Master Yourself and Master Your Life. Past, Present, and Future. The Power is Within You / Kyle C. Becker
Description: [Renton, Washington] : [Prosperity Now Life Coaching], [2021]
Identifiers: ISBN 978-17374732-0-6 (paperback) | ISBN 978-17374732-2-0 (hardback) | ISBN 978-1-7374732-1-3 (ebook)
Subjects: LCSH: Change (Psychology) | Self-actualization (Psychology) | Conduct of life. | Self-control. | LCGFT: Self-help publications.
Classification: LCC BF637.C4 B43 2021 (print) | LCC BF637.C4 (ebook) | DDC 158.1--dc23

For more information, contact: prosperitynowlifecoaching@gmail.com

CONTENTS

INTRODUCTION ... 1

PART ONE: MASTER YOURSELF

1. CREATE A BURNING DESIRE TO CHANGE ... 10
2. THE FEAR OF CHANGE ... 42
3. FOCUSING YOUR POWER TO CHANGE ... 51
4. THE PERSONAL INVENTORY ... 72
5. PART 1: THE FREEDOM TO CHANGE ... 92
6. PART 2: THE POWER TO CHANGE YOUR PAST ... 110
7. THE POWER TO CHANGE YOUR BEHAVIORS ... 126
8. YOUR IDEAL SELF ... 137
9. SELF MASTERY ... 158

PART TWO: MASTER YOUR LIFE

10. YOUR LIFE INTENTIONALLY ... 181
11. PLAN YOUR WORK ... 198
12. BREATHE LIFE INTO IT ... 214
13. THE QUALITY OF YOUR JOURNEY ... 225
14. YOU SHALL KNOW YOUR TRUTH ... 240
15. YOUR TRUTH SHALL SET YOU FREE ... 260
16. YOUR OMEGA STATE ... 289
17. YOUR LIFE IS BUT A REFLECTION OF YOURSELF ... 315

APPENDIX A:

VISUALIZATION ENHANCEMENT EXERCISES ... 324

INTRODUCTION

Life doesn't give us what we want. It gives us what we are. If we want our lives to change, we must first change ourselves. If we want something different, then we must be different. If we want more, we must first become more.

There came a point in my life where to survive I needed to be willing to change everything about myself and my life. I was fighting a battle with alcoholism and losing. There was a rumor going around that I had a drinking problem. Everyone seemed to be in on it. My boss, my best friend, my brothers, my parents, my wife, my sons. My pride wouldn't allow me to accept it until it was too late. I suffered from alcoholism.

Alcoholism, a disease that has taken countless millions of lives and ruined countless millions of others, a disease that leaves its sufferers unable to stop drinking no matter how much they try or how much they want to quit. It's a progressive disease, which means it only gets worse and worse. Slowly but surely it takes a person's body and mind, destroying their life in the process.

The final nine months of my drinking left me frustrated and broken on a daily basis, as all I wanted to do was to not drink for that day, and every day I ended up at home with a bottle, dumbfounded. All I wanted to do was quit, and I seemed powerless to do so.

I had chosen the bottle over a seventeen-year marriage, breaking up a family of four. I had lost my health, was fifty pounds overweight; I had begun bruising all over my body and was lying to others about their origins. I was calling in sick to work on a weekly basis with a variety of fictitious health issues. My employer was growing impatient. I was on the verge of losing my job and my house and living a life that I didn't want to live, and I was powerless to do anything about it.

The night of my last drink, I had succumbed to my disease once again. I woke up committed to not drink that day. All day it was a battle cry in my mind of how this was going to be the day. If I could get one day sober then I could get two. And from there I could make my drinking habit a sober habit. But I was powerless. Driving home that day, focused on just getting home without a bottle, I ended up in a grocery store parking lot. In that parking lot I pleaded with myself to "Just go home Kyle. Don't go in the store. If you don't buy a bottle you won't drink today." Ending up in the store saying to myself, "Just get back in your car. What are you doing!?!? You don't want this, Kyle!" Ending up at home with the bottle, I found the power to pour that bottle out without drinking it. And that's when the insanity of the first drink owned me. There was a feeling that if I didn't drink I would die. A deep physical pain gnawed at me, telling me that my world was going to catch fire if I didn't have that drink. I ended up going to a different store and buying a bottle.

A couple hours later, after drinking that bottle of vodka, I sat a chair down in front of my then seventeen-year-old son and told him that I couldn't stop drinking, and if I didn't get help I was afraid I was going to drink myself to death. The look on his face, the shame in my heart, was too much to bear.

I went up to my bedroom and called everyone I could think of. No one answered. I was panicked and so very afraid. I went into my bathroom and curled up into a ball on the floor. So scared. So tired of fighting. Crying that cry that burns but makes no sound. Lying on my bathroom floor, broken, my disease had taken all that I was. Every time I had told myself "This is the last drink! I will never do this again!" and ended up drinking anyway, I lost a little bit of myself. My futile attempt at quitting drinking was like trying to stop a freight train by throwing a handful of sand at it. There was nothing I could do. Lying there, I played the reel forward. I couldn't stop drinking. It was progressively getting worse. I had lost some things that I didn't want to lose, and the disease was about to take a great deal more. I was a man I didn't want to be, living a life I didn't want to live, and deathly afraid that I would die some horrible alcoholic death.

In that moment, burning, crying that kind of cry that makes no sound, I became willing to do whatever it takes to not be that man any longer... to not live that life. To not die that death.

I had to be willing to evolve and grow no matter how difficult it was or how much pain I had to walk through.

I had to reach that moment of surrender. That moment of willingness to do whatever it takes for as long as it takes to not be that person any longer and not live that life. I had to be willing to change everything. In that willingness to change everything I have gained everything. I hope this book will help you find that same willingness.

If you are reading this book, it means there is something about yourself or your life you want to change. No matter how big or small that change is, please know that you are in the right place. It means you have this feeling inside that there is more to life than this. That you are capable of, and meant for, so much more than you are getting. You may have tried different techniques. You may have tried "thinking" your way out of your situation and failed. You may not have all the answers right now. And that's ok. The answers will come. You are exactly who and where you are supposed to be, exactly at this moment. It doesn't matter what your life has been like up to this point. This book will help you increase the quality of it in every way. All the power you will ever need lies within you. This book will help you find it, develop it, and master it. This program will always work when you work it. If you are ready to put in the work, willing to become the most magnificent version of yourself, and begin to live the life of your dreams, then read on.

In this book, you will learn skills and techniques to improve your life in every conceivable way. You will learn to use techniques from Neuro Linguistic Programming (NLP). You will use those techniques to enhance visualization exercises that are in harmony with the law of attraction. And you will learn proven character-building techniques from proven twelve step programs to become not only the best version of yourself but the best version of yourself that you consciously choose to become. You will be given the tools and the power to intentionally create yourself in whatever image you like. You will be given the tools and power to intentionally become the person you want to become.

What you've purchased is really two books. One on Self Mastery (Part 1) and one on Life Mastery (Part 2). There are a couple of ways you can approach this book. If you just want to read through it and don't do any of the exercises, you will gain a great deal of awareness and knowledge into why you and your life are the way they are right now. With this awareness you will be able to make great strides in your life. If you decide to read it and do the activities, you will begin to become the master of yourself and the master of your life. Either way, you will benefit greatly from what you are about to read. Sometimes I just read through this book. Sometimes I do the exercises depending on what my current situation needs. But I continue to do the work and I continue to grow from it.

IN PART 1 OF THIS BOOK, "MASTER YOURSELF," YOU WILL LEARN TO:

- Create a burning desire to change. You will create the force necessary to make a beginning of it.

- Recognize how fear has been affecting every area of your life and learn how to overcome fear and remove this insidious roadblock from your life.

- Free up the energy and power trapped in your past so you can focus it on the present and the future.

- Uncover the unresolved moments of your past, discover the lessons and growth they hold for you, and discard any unwanted elements still causing you pain.

- Consciously create and install resourceful behaviors and responses to life, replacing your unresourceful behaviors and reactions to life and giving you complete control over how you show up in life.

- Design your ideal self and create a simple and time-efficient daily program that will help you accelerate your journey to becoming your ideal self.

- With the power of Timeline Cleansing and Timeline

Reimprinting, you have the power to use all the moments of your life so you can increase the quality of every area of your life; past, present, and future.

- Gain conscious control over your fears, beliefs, thoughts, emotions, behaviors, reactions, and responses to life.

IN PART 2, "MASTER YOUR LIFE," YOU WILL LEARN TO:

- Stop living life by default and live your life with intention and definitive purpose. You will learn how to turn your thoughts into things. You will learn how to consciously create the circumstances and life you want to create.

- Consciously create an ideal for every area of your life and create an achievable plan to realize those ideals. Action is required for change. If nothing changes, then nothing changes.

- Consciously and powerfully create the life of your dreams, putting life on notice that you will not be denied.

- Enjoy every step of your journey. Find joy, peace, fulfillment, and prosperity, now. It is all about the quality of the journey and the person you become along the way.

- Uncover your beliefs and personal truths that govern your life in every way, overcome any unwanted or limiting beliefs, and adopt the beliefs to complete your journey.

- Create your Omega state, that embodiment of the

best you that you can imagine and learn to be that person now.

- Be invited in the last chapter to take it to the next level. Now that your eyes have been opened to the possibilities of you, you will be invited to continue to evolve into something altogether more.

- Push the limits of what you believe you are capable of and the person you believe you can become.

HOW TO USE THIS BOOK FOR BEST RESULTS

- Read "Appendix A – Visualizations Exercises." This will serve a dual purpose of increasing your ability to create detailed images and environments in your mind and will also increase the quality of your subjective experience of your life now.

- Access and print all the worksheets in this book on my website: www.yourpowertochange.com. There are copies in this book, which will absolutely serve their necessary purpose, but I find it much more powerful to have it in workbook form as well.

- Complete the exercises and chapters in the order they are written. All the skills and techniques were meant to build upon each other. They start off slow, giving you a chance to learn the fundamentals, then increase in power as your proficiency grows. You must learn to crawl before you walk, and walk before you run.

- Start a *Power to Change* journal. You will be asked to do some writing and brainstorming. I will also ask you to write things down on a separate piece of paper quite often. Keeping it all together in one place will allow you to access the information you need at any time.

- Repetition, repetition, repetition. Many of these skills and techniques will require practice for you to become proficient with them. Some will act to "wire" or install programmed responses into your subconscious mind. This will allow you to respond in a resourceful manner where you used to react in an unresourceful manner. The key to wiring these programs is repetition, speed, and intensity.

You are reading the right book. Now is the time to make it happen. In order to get more out of life, all you need to do is BECOME MORE. This book will help you do just that.

PART ONE

MASTER YOURSELF

CHAPTER 1

CREATE A BURNING DESIRE TO CHANGE

*"Desire is the starting point of all achievement,
not a hope, not a wish, but a keen pulsating desire which
transcends everything."*

~ NAPOLEON HILL

How do I get to that place where I'm ready to do what it takes for as long as it takes to live the life I want to live?

How can I begin to believe that I can change?

How can I stop making resolutions and start making changes?

How can I hold myself accountable to and follow through on the promises I make to myself?

What is it that gives someone the courage to say "no" to

a life of quiet desperation and become willing to do whatever it takes to not live that life anymore?

What inspires someone to step away from the safety and predictability of that life in exchange for the life they have always dreamed of living?

It is these questions and more that we will cover in this chapter.

Change is a verb. It is action. Merriam-Webster defines change as "to alter, vary, modify, mean to be different..." Albert Einstein said, "The definition of insanity is doing the same thing over and over, but expecting different results." In this chapter, you will begin a journey that will last a lifetime. You will live your life with intention and purpose. You will take the steps necessary to change. You will act.

In this chapter you will begin to recognize the areas of your life and the things about yourself that you need and want to change, and you will come to make a decision to change those things. You will also identify things in yourself and in your life, those things that are not currently present but you would like to have more of. Sounds familiar, right? But recognizing the need for change, and deciding to change, will never bring about change. Only action will bring about change. It is my hope that by the end of this chapter, you have a clear idea of what you want to change, that you will decide to make those changes, and that you develop a burning desire that will motivate you to act and bring about that change.

I want you to feel good when you read this book. I want you to feel like there is newfound hope in your life and begin to believe that there is a way to be the person you want to be, and live the life you want to live. I want you to feel that spark within yourself. That wonderful, bright, powerful, and mighty feeling of being alive again. Motivated. Inspired. Driven. I want you to begin to feel that there's nothing that you cannot accomplish. That you have the power within yourself to truly and actually begin to move the mountains in your life. To get past the obstacles that have always stopped you. To truly become more. But to change we must be willing to act differently. We must be willing to walk through whatever we need to walk through in order to achieve that which we set out to achieve. We must find that fire within ourselves that will get us moving and driving forward no matter what.

To act, we must first develop a burning desire to do so. We must reach that point where not to act is no longer acceptable. The bigger the change to be made, and the greater the fear you need to overcome, the greater your desire to act must be.

In 1964, famed civil rights activist Fannie Lou Hamer said, "My whole life, I have been sick and tired. Now I am sick and tired of being sick and tired." She recognized the need for change. She decided she wanted to be that change. And she reached that ever-important point of no return where she began to do the things she needed to do to enact changes in herself and in her life. And in doing so she was an instrument of positive change in a society that sorely needed it, and in the lives and opinions of countless millions of people all across the world.

This statement sums up that powerful and unstoppable shift in her consciousness that has been adopted and used by countless twelve-step programs and personal growth programs across the world, to describe the mindset of "enough is enough." To create that desire to act. To empower millions of people to draw that line in the sand and say, "No more! I am not going to live like this any longer! I am not going to live this life anymore!" Whether you want to lose weight, change a career, get out of a bad relationship, or gain freedom from life-threatening addictions and situations, no matter what you want to change, you need to get to a point where you can say, with complete conviction, "Enough is enough! No more!" That you are sick and tired of being sick and tired. That you will no longer settle for good when you know you were meant to be great. That you will no longer accept your current situation as being your fate in life. You will decide to do whatever it takes for as long as it takes to become the person you want to be so you can live the life you want to live. It's at this point where your quality of consciousness will begin to change for the better. This is ground zero. This is your new beginning.

My ground zero was lying on that bathroom floor, broken and desperate, needing to change so badly but not knowing how I possibly could. I couldn't stop drinking. I was overweight and unhealthy. I was on the verge of failing in my career. My relationships had suffered greatly, and I didn't know how I could possibly be forgiven for the things I had done and said. On the inside I was insecure and afraid. My self-esteem was beaten up badly from my countless failings and I had no self-confidence left whatsoever. By applying the principles and activities I am about to share with you I was able to make a new beginning. I have stopped drinking altogether. I am as healthy as I have ever been. My career took off and soared to amazing heights. I love myself today exactly as I am. Imperfections and all. The fear that ran my life is, for the most part, gone. And all the moments of my life have been forgiven. It has taken years of work, but all the moments of my life have been forgiven. I did the work and all the regrets and resentments that I held onto for so long have left me. All that remains is love and appreciation for all that was and is. Words are feeble attempts to describe the level of humility and gratitude this has given me. Tears of joy wet my face as I write this. I am so very grateful and humbled by it.

EXERCISE: LIGHT THE FIRE OF CHANGE
The exercises in this book will increase your understanding and awareness and control of your past, present, and future. You will be asked to describe your memories and your dreams, which will show you how your consciousness is actually coding and storing them. Do the best you can on these exercises. Apply yourself. Remember, thinking about change will not change your life. Recognizing your need to change will not change your life. Only action will change your life.

Imagine you have one year left to live. Imagine looking back on your life from that perspective. We have heard this and been told that this perspective will help motivate us to change. And to some extent it has, and it will. Typically though, we get caught up in the inertia of our lives and fall back into the same habits and situations. Those few moments of reflection are lacking the power needed to reach exit velocity from the life we are currently living. For the remainder of this chapter, we will apply the power of NLP or Neuro Linguistic Programming to this end-of-life reflection exercise and find the power needed to get out of whatever rut we are in and begin to become the person we want to become so we can live the life we want to live. For the remainder of this chapter, you will begin to develop your burning desire to act.

WHAT IS NEURO LINGUISTIC PROGRAMMING (NLP)?
NLP is the study of our subjective experience of reality. It's built on the premise that people react and respond to their

own subjective map of reality and not to reality itself. That we view life through our own unique lens that is colored and distorted by all the sensory input we have experienced up to that moment and our opinions and interpretations of those experiences. Basically, we all see life differently. Everything in life will be experienced differently by everyone else because everyone has had a different set of experiences up to that point. Every moment will mean something different to everyone else because everyone has experienced a different set of moments up to that point.

NLP was first created as a therapeutic method to help people overcome psychological difficulties in a very short time. Some of the top therapists were modeled, namely famed psychologist Virginia Satir and hypnotherapy pioneer Milton Erickson. They were referred to as miracle workers in their fields. People that had gone to therapists for the same reason for years without significant changes to their problems were able to find fast and lasting change through the techniques and exercises employed by Satir and Erickson. These techniques and exercises are the foundation of NLP.

In the same way that you don't need an advanced degree in electrical engineering or physics to turn a light on or microwave your dinner, and you don't need to understand quantum physics to use your smartphone, you do not need to be a certified NLP practitioner, psychologist, or hypnotherapist to use some very basic NLP techniques to bring about staggering changes in your life.

I will ask you to do some work now. To open your mind and learn new skills. I will now challenge you to take that first step. I will invite you to act. Nothing in life worth having will come to you without working for it. Nothing in life happens by accident. Your life now is a direct reflection of who you have been over the totality of all the moments of your life. All your thoughts. Your feelings. Your beliefs. Decisions. Actions. Reactions. All those things added together equal your life today. You see, if you keep doing the same things you have always done, you will continue to get the results you have always received. You get out of life what you put into it. What you put into life is who and what you are. Become more. Rise up. Elevate yourself. Remember why you are doing this. Remember why you searched for a book like this. Remember the discontent. Remember the hope. Remember your fears. Remember the joy. Remember the pain. Remember your dreams. Whatever your reason for wanting to change yourself and your life, bring it into your mind and your heart now. The rest of your life depends on what you choose to do, or choose not to do, next.

We will use four basic NLP techniques in this book. VAKOG, Perceptual Positions, Anchoring, and Timeline work. In that order, with some basic NLP philosophy throughout. This is very simple to learn; anyone can do it. And the results you will get from using these techniques will be astonishingly fast and lasting. You will use these tools in conjunction with many others to become more, to increase your level of consciousness by gaining control of and increasing your conscious and subconscious experience of reality.

ACTION AND LEARNING

I will introduce you to more NLP techniques as you progress. Like any exercise routine, if you do not do the work, you will see no results. The techniques I will teach you in this chapter are fundamental and will be the bedrock of every NLP technique you will learn and use. With these techniques, you can decide how you want to respond in any situation. With these techniques, you can intentionally and deliberately live the life you want to live.

VAKOG—THE BUILDING BLOCKS OF YOUR EXPERIENCE OF REALITY

A key skill you will learn is the ability to remember and imagine situations in great detail. You will do this by bringing as much sensory information into these real and imagined situations as possible. Appendix A has some good exercises to help you increase your ability to do this. Our memories are structured using this sensory information. We structure our experience of reality and our memories with the five senses. We will be referring to these senses as modalities.

- **Visual** (what you saw)
- **Auditory** (what you heard)
- **Kinesthetic** (what you felt, physically and emotionally)
- **Olfactory** (what you smelled)
- **Gustatory** (what you tasted)

Everyone experiences these modalities differently and has a preferred modality they are strongest in and use the most. The three primary modalities are visual, auditory, and kinesthetic. For our purposes, we will be working primarily with these three. If you have a strong sense of smell or taste, feel free to add those to any exercise.

SUBMODALITIES

Each modality has its own unique structure called submodalities. Submodalities are not concerned with the content of the experience or memory, but the structure and qualities of how we experience it. Below is a list of common submodalities.

- **Visual-** Location of image, size, is it framed like a TV or panoramic, black and white or color, moving or still, associated (seeing through your eyes) or dissociated (seeing as if a neutral observer).
- **Auditory-** Volume, Speed, Location, Tonality
- **Kinesthetic-** Location of feeling, shape, movement, pressure, color, directional spin

This is how we store, or code, every memory we have. This is how we subjectively perceive our reality.

SUB-MODALITIES CHECKLIST

VISUAL - HOW YOU SEE IT	DESCRIPTION
Size of Image	
Black and White or Color	
Moving or Still	
Associated or Dissociated	
Framed or Panoramic	
Location	
AUDITORY - HOW YOU HEAR IT	
Location	
Direction	
Internal or External	
Loud or Soft	
Fast or Slow	
High pitch or low pitch	
KINESTHETIC - HOW YOU FEEL IT	
Location of Sensation	
Size of Sensation	
Shape of Sensation	
Movement of Sensation	
Vibration of Sensation	
Pressure of Sensation	
Temperature of Sensation	
Weight or Density of Sensation	
What you would name this sensation	
Your posture and breathing	

ALTERING SUBMODALITIES

In this book, you will learn to change and control your beliefs, fears, thoughts, emotions, and behaviors by controlling and changing their modalities and submodalities. The greater detail you have for each situation, the greater your ability to influence it.

There are many ways that changing the submodalities of a memory can change the meaning of a memory, experience, or event. Here are some examples:

Visual- By changing the location of the image, or decreasing or increasing its size, or changing it to color or black and white, or making it closer or further away, or making it brighter or dimmer, or making it a still picture or adding movement to it, or making it clearer or less focused, associating or dissociating, etc.

Auditory- By making it louder or quieter, making it faster or slower, changing where you hear it in your head or what direction it is coming from, making it higher pitched or lower pitched, making it smooth or choppy, changing the voice altogether to one of a cartoon or famous person, etc.

Kinesthetic- Changing the location of the feeling, changing the shape, adding, changing, or taking away movement, adding or decreasing pressure, changing its color, changing the directional spin, size of spin, or speed of spin, etc.

ASSOCIATION/DISSOCIATION

Being associated in a memory or visualization means you see this moment through your own eyes. You hear through your own ears, and feel what you are feeling in the remembered or imagined moment. When we associate with a memory, we allow ourselves to experience the kinesthetic (feelings, emotions, etc.) of the situation to a much greater degree.

Being dissociated in a memory or visualization means you are witnessing yourself from the position of a neutral observer. Like a fly on the wall. This isn't always easy at first, but it will get easier with practice. Dissociating allows you to step out of your body, which allows you to set aside the kinesthetic elements of the situation. This is especially true of the emotional components, which gives you a fresh perspective on the situation. So much of our thinking is affected by our emotions. When we change our emotions, we change our thinking.

Everyone's responses to these submodality changes will be different. Typically, when you increase something, make it bigger or louder, you increase the intensity of the memory. This can be good or bad, depending on whether the memory is good or bad. Through practice, this will become an intuitive process for you. You will find that just by altering the submodalities, you can change the meaning of your memories, including the emotions created by those memories. You will be given many opportunities to do this throughout this book, but nothing is stopping you from doing this now. Play around with it. If you do not like the results of your changes, then you can simply change them back.

Be patient with yourself as you proceed through this book and learn these new techniques. As you practice the techniques you will learn, and you will get better at them. The better you get at them, the more profound the effect they have on your life will be. With these techniques, you can change your subjective experience of reality consciously, intentionally, and deliberately. Think of them as tools you can put in your toolbox to be used when appropriate. You will use these tools to build a better you, build a better life, and if you want to, build a better world.

DESIRED OUTCOME WORKSHEET

Desired Outcome	How do you see it?	How do you hear it?	How do you feel it?	How does it affect the ones you love?

PART 1: DESIRED OUTCOME

This is where we start doing a little work. If you knew you could not fail, what would you endeavor to do? What this question does is suspend the fear of failure and the fear of change, putting them on the shelf if you will; this allows you to look at the possibilities of your life. It is time to allow yourself to imagine your ideal life. To allow yourself to dream.

The first thing to focus on is your desired change or desired outcome. The Desired Outcome worksheet on the adjacent page will help you get specific about the life you want to live and the person you want to become. The things you put on this sheet could be anything from desired living situations, relationships, careers, financial situation, health aspects, weight issues, character traits, beliefs, mindsets; anything at all you can think about that you would like to change. Sometimes it's just one, or maybe two things. Some people change everything about their life. There is no right or wrong way. What this whole book is about is helping you live your life your way. In as many life categories as you want to, write out the ideal for your life. What is the desired outcome of the change you want to make in each area of your life?

The key to this is imagining the change as having happened already, as if you are experiencing it in the current moment. List what you see, hear, and feel and any of the submodalities of those senses as you can. The clearer it is, the more you will believe that it can be. Our subconscious mind cannot distinguish between real or imagined experiences. Especially if these experiences have an intense kinesthetic (emotional) quality to them. We will cover this in great depth in the chapters to come.

Thoroughness is key. Take time to search your mind and soul for what you want. Suspend all fear. Set aside self-doubt. If fear or doubt creep in, just tell yourself that you are just dreaming. You are totally safe. Allow yourself to dream like you did when you were a little kid, before life told you what was and was not possible for you.

YOUR POWER TO CHANGE

CURRENT SITUATION WORKSHEET

Current Situation	How do you see it?	How do you hear it?	How do you feel it?	How does it affect the ones you love?

PART 2: CURRENT SITUATION

Now that you have a better idea of what you want and where you want to go, it's time to figure out where you currently are. Write these on the Current Situation worksheet on the adjacent page. Ask yourself, "Where am I currently at in my life relative to these desired outcomes?" Honesty and objectivity are crucial in this part; seeing things as they truly are. Make no excuses for anyone involved. Your answers to these questions help you see your situation more clearly. To see past excuses and blame and fear and see things as they are. Fill out all the columns in the worksheet as thoroughly as possible.

- What does the current situation look like?
- What does my self-talk sound like in this situation?
- How do I feel about it?
- What emotions am I feeling?
- How has it negatively affected me and the people around me?

Now that you have described your situation, what you do and do not want, consider your life again. Is there anything else you would like to change? Even if you don't know what you would like as an alternative, write it down anyway. You don't need to know what the solution or the answer is. If the desire is there, the solution will surely come. You can put these on the Current Situation worksheet and apply the process to them.

ALTERNATIVE PERSPECTIVE WORKSHEET

Desired Outcome or Current Situation	Dissociated or neutral position experience and notes	Associated as the "other person" experience and notes	Associated with self again. Any changes or new insights?	Any changes you need to make to what you want or do not want?

PART 3: ALTERNATIVE PERSPECTIVES

This is the Alternative Perspectives technique. It's meant to help you deepen your understanding of a situation as well as discover different options and alternatives that are not available from your current viewpoint. Whenever we make changes in our lives, it's wise to evaluate the situation from as many perspectives as possible. As they say in the carpentry profession, measure twice and cut once. Make sure the change you make is the change you really want.

Please use the Alternative Perspectives worksheet on the adjacent page to do your work.

Step 1. Apply this process to the desired outcome first, and the current situation second. Fully associate into each one. See what you see. Hear what you hear. Feel what you feel. Think what you think. Immerse yourself in it.

Step 2. Next, dissociate from the situation. See yourself in the desired outcome and current situation from the viewpoint of a neutral observer. See each as if you were a complete stranger and knew nothing about the situation you are observing, except for what you are observing. Ask yourself these questions. Take the time necessary to allow the answers to come:

- How would I describe what I am observing?
- Knowing nothing about the person I am looking at, what advice would I give them?
- What do I make of their current situation and their desired outcomes?
- Is there any other insight that is coming to me through this?

Again, allow these questions some time to answer themselves. Allow insight and inspiration to happen.

Step 3. If there is another human or humans involved and affected by your desired outcome or current situation, you can imagine yourself in their position as well. See what they see. Hear what they hear. Feel what they feel. Rise up out of yourself and settle down into and as them. Once settled, take some time to pull into your awareness, everything you know about them, and what has happened in their life. Their perspective is the sum of all the experiences of their life. The more thorough you are with this the better. It will really take you out of yourself. Ask yourself the same questions.

- What do I see from this position?
- Knowing what I know about this person I am looking at (you), what advice would I give them?
- What do I make of their desired outcome and current situation?
- Is there any other insight coming through this?
- What am I thinking and what am I feeling?

Allow these questions some time to answer themselves. Allow insight and inspiration to happen.

Step 4. Allow yourself to experience everything in your desired outcome and current situation again in the first person. See what you see. Hear what you hear. Feel what you feel.

- What have you learned from this exercise?
- What has changed?

If this added insight has changed anything for you, make the appropriate changes to your Desired Outcome and Current Situation worksheets.

THE ULTIMATE PERSPECTIVE WORKSHEET

Desired Outcome or Current Situation	How you see it, hear it, feel it. Sub-modalities	Can you change the experience by changing the sub-modalities?	What are you grateful for most, or what do you regret the most?	How has it affected your whole life?

PART 4: THE ULTIMATE PERSPECTIVE

Now it's time to tie this all together. By now, hopefully, you have a much clearer, broader, and deeper understanding of where you currently are and where you want to go. The first part of the following exercise is not about morbid reflection or beating yourself up. It brings you closer to that feeling of "Enough is enough! No more!" It lights the fire for change within you. You can wait until you are fed up with the current situation or you can intentionally accelerate the process. That is what this exercise is meant to do.

Please review the Ultimate Perspective worksheet on the adjacent page.

I will ask you now to travel in time to the end of your life and view your current situation from the ultimate perspective. The perspective of all the moments of your life, past, present, and future. This is not an exercise to be rushed. The more patient and thorough you are, the more profound the effect it will have on your life.

Imagine yourself at the end of your life. You have only a week left to live. Step into and fully associate as your future-self. See what your future-self sees. Feel what you feel. Hear what you hear. The more detailed this is, the more powerful this technique is. See. Hear. Feel. Think. Spend some time here.

Starting with the Current Situation worksheet, go through each situation you have listed. With each situation, pause, consider these ideas, and allow yourself the time to consider them. To contemplate and ponder them. To really grasp the gravity of the situation and all its potential implications.

- How has this negatively affected your life up to the point of your writing this?

- If nothing changes, how will this affect the rest of your life?
- What will happen if it gets worse?
- How will it affect the people you love?
- What will not happen if you do not make a change?
- At the end of your life, how will you feel about not making a change?
- What will you regret not being able to experience because of not making this change?

Notice how you are experiencing this future moment. What words would you use to describe it? What do you see, hear, feel, and what are you thinking? Now write down any submodalities that you can recognize.

- **Visual-** Location of image, size, is it framed like a TV or panoramic, black and white or color, moving or still, associated (seeing through your eyes) or dissociated (seeing as if a neutral observer)
- **Auditory-** Volume, Speed, Location, Tonality
- **Kinesthetic-** Location of feeling, shape, movement, pressure, color

Now ask yourself these questions:

"Is there anything I can do to change the submodalities of this moment that will help me make the changes I need to make? Can I change something about the way I see, hear, feel, experience, or think in this moment that will help me make the changes that I need to make?

Refer back to the Altering Submodalities section earlier in this chapter if needed.

Again, "Is there anything I can do to change the submodalities of this moment that will help me make the changes that I need to make? Can I change something about the way I see, hear, feel, experience, or think in this moment that will help me make the changes that I need to make?"

You should listen to your intuition on this one. It's ok if nothing comes to mind. Relax your conscious mind, be here now, and listen. Allow your whole consciousness to work on this for you. This question will mean what it needs to mean to you, and everything will be exactly as it is supposed to be. There is no right or wrong way to respond to this question.

Remember how you feel right now. Allow yourself to believe that your past does not equal your future. Say it out loud to yourself. If you don't believe it, then imagine that you do. Ask yourself "What would it be like if I believed that my past does not equal my future?" Believe that you have the power to change. Believe that the rest of your life can be everything that you want it to be.

Before you do the next part of the exercise, take a break. Take a walk, eat some food, take a nap, watch some TV. Allow this portion of the exercise the necessary time to breathe and do whatever it is that it needs to do.

Now going back to the future, you have a week left to live, consider the desired outcome worksheet. Pause and allow yourself to consider these ideas. To contemplate and ponder them. To grasp the gravity of the situation and all its potential implications. Write your answers to the below questions on the worksheet at the end of the chapter.

- How has changing this situation positively affected the rest of your life?
- Imagine all the things this change has allowed you to do.
- Imagine all the possibilities this change has created for you.
- In what ways has this positive change affected the people you love?
- In what ways has this positive change affected your community and any charities or causes you would like to make a difference in?

At the end of your life, how will it feel to not have any regrets? To know that you have lived the life you wanted to live. To have become the person you wanted to become. To be filled with the feeling of peace, and hope, and fulfillment. To experience the joy that comes from a life well lived.

Notice how you are experiencing this future moment. What words would you use to describe it? What do you see, hear, feel, and what are you thinking? Now write down any submodalities that you can recognize.

- **Visual-** Location of image, size, is it framed like a TV or panoramic, black and white or color, moving or still, associated (seeing through your eyes) or dissociated (seeing as if a neutral observer)
- **Auditory-** Volume, Speed, Location, Tonality
- **Kinesthetic-** Location of feeling, shape, movement, pressure, color

Now ask yourself these questions:

"Is there anything I can do to change the submodalities of this moment that will help me make the changes that I need to make? Can I change something about the way I see, hear, feel, experience, or think in this moment that will help me make the changes that I need to make?"

Again, refer back to the Altering Submodalities section earlier in this chapter if needed.

Again, you should listen to your intuition on this one. It's ok if nothing comes to mind. Relax your conscious mind, be here now, and listen. Allow your whole consciousness to work on this for you. This question will mean what it needs to mean to you, and everything will be exactly as it is supposed to be. There is no right or wrong way to respond to this question.

Again, "Is there anything I can do to change the submodalities of this moment that will help me make the changes that I need to make? Can I change something about the way I see, hear, feel, experience, or think in this moment that will help me make the changes that I need to make?"

If you have been honest and thorough in this chapter, you will have come up with quite a few things you would like to change in yourself and change in your life. You have begun to develop a burning desire to change. I know that looking at your work thus far, you may be thinking there is far too much to do and wondering where you should possibly start. The answer is simple:

> "A journey of a thousand miles
> starts with a single step."

If all you do in this book, and you will hear me say this throughout the book, is do the activities in this chapter with all that you are and have, you will have profoundly changed yourself and your life for the better. I will repeat. If you do this chapter well, you will see huge changes in yourself and your life. All of the exercises in this book are like that. Life-changing.

Before you move on to the next chapter, you need to take that first step. Otherwise, all you are doing is reading another book on change and thinking about change. It's time to act. What is one small positive change you can make today that will move you toward becoming the person you want to become and living the life you want to live?

Whatever the answer is, and no matter how small that change may seem to you, make that change. Make that change now. Whether that's researching nutrition, listing things to do to start a business, taking that first walk you've been meaning to take, or making that phone call or sending that email you have been putting off. It doesn't matter what it is. Take that first step. Life cannot guide you if you are standing still. By taking the first step, you are putting life on notice. It doesn't matter in what direction you take that step. Just take the first step. Make one small positive change today.

The night of my last drink, after I had summoned the courage to call my family and ask for help, my first step was to research inpatient and outpatient rehabilitation facilities. I made a list. I sent out some feelers. The very next day, I received a call from a facility letting me know that they had a bed that just opened up and that they would accept me. This was huge for me, because if I didn't act on this soon it just would have been more of the same. If I hadn't acted then, I may not have ever gotten sober. If I hadn't acted in that moment, I may not have been here today to write this sentence.

Now that you have a better understanding of what you do and do not want and you are armed with a sincere desire and willingness to change, how do you go about making these changes? You may be asking yourself if making these changes are even possible and if you have the power to make these changes. In the next chapter, we will discuss the main roadblock standing between you and your dreams. That roadblock is fear.

SUB-MODALITIES CHECKLIST

VISUAL - HOW YOU SEE IT	DESCRIPTION
Size of Image	
Black and White or Color	
Moving or Still	
Associated or Dissociated	
Framed or Panoramic	
Location	
AUDITORY - HOW YOU HEAR IT	
Location	
Direction	
Internal or External	
Loud or Soft	
Fast or Slow	
High pitch or low pitch	
KINESTHETIC - HOW YOU FEEL IT	
Location of Sensation	
Size of Sensation	
Shape of Sensation	
Movement of Sensation	
Vibration of Sensation	
Pressure of Sensation	
Temperature of Sensation	
Weight or Density of Sensation	
What you would name this sensation	
Your posture and breathing	

CHAPTER 1 KEY TAKEAWAYS

- Thinking about change and deciding to change never changed a thing. Only action creates change. Change is a verb.
- Neuro Linguistic Programming, or NLP, is the science of our subjective experience of reality. NLP will help you change your beliefs, thoughts, emotions, behaviors, actions, and reactions.
- The more you practice these techniques, the better you will get at them.
- The bigger the change, the stronger the desire to change must be.
- You can increase your understanding, awareness, and options by looking at a situation from multiple different perspectives.
- You can accelerate becoming "sick and tired of being sick and tired" and increase your desire to change by experiencing your life through the Ultimate Perspective.
- A journey of a thousand miles begins with a single step. Take that single step today. Act now. Make the change in your reality real. Put the universe on notice that you will not be denied.

CHAPTER 2

THE FEAR OF CHANGE

"Fear defeats more people than
any other one thing in the world."

~ RALPH WALDO EMERSON

For most of my life, I have lived with and been influenced by fear. Some were subtle forms of fear like being shy and not asking out the girl I had a crush on, and some were major forms of fear, like the fear of speaking in front of an audience. Fear has manifested itself in many ways in my life. The fear that I wasn't good enough. The fear that I would someday be cast aside and abandoned. The fear that if you knew who I truly was, or if I was not who I thought you wanted me to be, that you would reject me. The fear that I was stuck in my current career and wasn't good enough to do anything else. The fear that my employer would finally figure out that they didn't need me and that I'm not as good as they thought I was. The fear that the wonderful life I had built would be taken away from me. The fear that I would one day be alone. The fear that I would fail as a father and let my children down. The fear of either losing something I thought I needed to feel happy and safe, or not receiving something that I thought I needed to feel happy and safe. Not that I didn't experience any good moments, because I have lived a life full of blessings. But there was always this underlying feeling of insecurity that kept me in a constant state of needing to be in control, but never truly feeling like I was. To one degree or another, fear has decreased the quality of every area of my life.

By working the program I will provide for you in this book, I overcame my fears and replaced them with peace, joy, serenity, hope, confidence, faith, humility, and gratitude. Becoming aware of my fears and how they were manifesting in my life was a game-changer for me, and I know it will be for you as well.

One of the biggest obstacles you will need to overcome to become the person you want to become and live the life of your dreams is fear. One of the main things holding you back is not some uncontrollable external force or circumstance. It is your fears and limiting beliefs that have been holding you back on your journey. To become the master of yourself, and become the master of your life, you must first learn to master your fears. In this book, you will learn many techniques that will help you to not only master fear but live a life without fear.

All fears are, to one degree or another, a perceived threat to our survival. When we are in survival mode, our subconscious mind exerts its unfathomable power into keeping us safe no matter what. Everything else is secondary, including our happiness and success in life. The more fear we eliminate from our lives, the more we can focus the power of our subconscious mind on our happiness and success. The less we need to survive, the more we can thrive. All the techniques and exercises in this book are meant to eliminate fear from your life and give you conscious control over your subconscious mind.

This chapter gives you a basic awareness and understanding of fear and how it has been affecting your life. It will help you to understand that most types of fear and almost all the fears that hold us back in life are not real. That they are a figment of our overprotective imagination. That fear stands for "False Evidence Appearing Real." In this chapter, we will shine the light of awareness on the subject of fear. It is my hope that this will arm you with the belief that fear is something that you can control and overcome.

To overcome fear, you will need to learn the truth about fear; to see what fear is, where it comes from, the different types of fear, and the purpose of each type of fear. As your understanding and awareness of fear increases, so will your ability to control it and overcome it.

Fear is a good thing. That's right. The only reason we are here today as a species, and have evolved to our current state of being, is a healthy sense of fear. Without fear, we would not have survived. The lions, tigers, and bears would have eaten us. I know this sounds pretty funny now, but this was a very common and real danger in our not-so-distant past. This fear is often called instinctual fear or primal fear. These fears are made to protect and ensure the three prime instincts. The survival instinct, the sex instinct, and the social instinct. The fear of death, the fear of oblivion of self and species, and the fear of being cast out of the tribe, which would make it harder to procreate and survive. A list could be made that is much larger and more complicated than this. Fear can manifest itself in many ways. You do not need to understand them all to take control of and overcome your fear. A simple understanding of these ideas is all that you need. All other fears, as we will learn in later chapters, are based on perceived and often misperceived potential threats to these three prime instincts.

To overcome your fears, you need to first recognize them and how they have been and are manifesting in your life. Once you get better at recognizing your fears, you will begin to trace those fears back to the thoughts or events that triggered them. When you become aware of and understand what is triggering your fears, you can respond how you want to instead of reacting in a fearful way.

All fear starts with a conscious or subconscious trigger. This causes all fear. The effect of this fear manifests in many ways. The easiest to recognize is the emotional or physiological response. The physiological responses involved with fear are just fast, condensed, powerful, biological programs. They evolved to create the fastest, most effective responses to potentially life-threatening conditions. They are only in us now because our ancestors used them effectively to not get eaten by a lion, tiger, or bear. They survived, procreated, and they passed these programs along to us.

Think about it: One million years ago, we were not at the top of the food chain as we are today. The reality of being eaten by a predator was very real. For instance, in going about our business in the forest, we might hear rustling in the bushes. Now, if we choose to pause, take in all the variables, weigh any responses versus past situations, and then choose to act, we would have surely been eaten. The emotional response of fear, that powerful complex biological reaction, happens faster than we can think. It happens at a subconscious level. Before we know it or have time to consider what is happening, we are doing whatever we can do to get out of harm's way, safe and alive to see another day. This reaction is called the fight/flight/freeze response. It prepares your body to fight, flee, or hide by increasing adrenaline and cortisol, raising your heart rate and breathing rate, and taking blood away from the skin and moving it to the muscles, heart, and mind. It allows us to jump higher into a tree, run faster and longer, burrow under something heavy, and causes our perception of pain to decrease. Survival is priority number one. All other considerations become secondary.

So, this response has kept us alive and served us well thus far, though the threat of being eaten by a predator is obviously not a realistic threat anymore in the daily lives of the average human being. Yet when we perceive something as a threat, anything as a threat, be it to our life, our standing in society, or our standing in a relationship, we react with this fear response to one degree or another. We go one step further by creating a fear response by merely imagining situations that might be a threat. When we are in a state of fear, we stop thinking about what we want, what makes us happy, and how we want to act, and we think about staying safe and surviving. This is how our instinct to survive has been limiting our ability to thrive.

The other kind of fear, psychological fear, is the one stopping us from reaching our full potential and living the life of our dreams. Your dreams, your aspirations, your vision for yourself and your life, all lie on the other side of this fear.

Understanding why we have psychological fear and

becoming aware of its positive intentions will allow us to gain control over it, find alternatives to it, and overcome it. Understanding that psychological fear is not real will allow us to summon the courage to step out in faith and walk through our fears.

Psychological fear, or imagined fear, is just that. Imagined. It lives in a future that hasn't happened yet and may never happen. Psychological fear happens when we imagine a future event and the different ways it might not end well for us.

Take something like the fear of public speaking, which holds a lot of us back. I know a lot about this because I had to walk through the fear of public speaking in my life. A conversation with oneself might go something like this:

"I know the importance of this presentation. I am prepared, and I know that it will open up many doors for me if I do well. But what if they don't like what I have to say? What if they don't like me? What if I freeze up and they realize I'm not qualified to have this job? What if I screw up badly enough and it costs me my job? I'll lose my home, and my wife will leave me, and I'll be left all alone to survive in a cold, scary world. If I get cast out, the lions, tigers, and bears will surely eat me."

I know this sounds absurd, but we actually do this. To one degree or another, depending on the mental makeup of the individual, we consciously and unconsciously believe that these potential dangers will ultimately threaten our survival, sex, or social instinct. Because these three prime instincts are perceived as being threatened, our fight/flight/flee response is activated to protect us from this perceived potential danger. We get anxious. We can't think straight. We want to run and hide. In this state it's almost impossible to give a decent, well-thought-out presentation.

Another example of psychological fear is the fear of change. A conversation with oneself might sound something like this:

"I really don't like my job anymore. I have outgrown it and feel unfulfilled. I want to do something different. I have a dream that I would like to go after. I have a gift I would like to share with the world. But what happens if my dream doesn't pan out? At least my current job is paying my bills, keeping a roof over my head, and feeding me. If I decide to change what I do then I might not be able to pay my bills. I might not be able to keep a roof over my head. What would my friends and family think? What would people down at the social club think? I would be such a loser. They would surely abandon me. I would be left alone in this scary world, homeless and destitute. I better just settle for the job that I have. Sure, it sucks and I hate it, but at least I am safe and secure and alive."

Again, this is a bit of a stretch, but this is the process many of us have actually gone through. Fear of change manifests as "good is the enemy of great," which also would translate to "Ok is the enemy of good," and "merely surviving is the enemy of ok." "Better the devil you know than the devil you do not know." These sayings are based on the fear that the unknown future will be worse than anything we are experiencing now. That if I change, it may make matters worse. It is a belief we have that "No matter how good or bad my life is, I am still alive, and it hasn't killed me yet." The fear of change hinders our growth, keeps us stuck, makes us accept bad situations, and causes much suffering and pain. It is a human tendency to seek routine. To seek predictability. To control the variables to ensure our safety and security. Too often, the walls we build to protect ourselves become a prison.

One more example of psychological fear, of which there are many, is the fear of being alone. A conversation with oneself might go something like this:

"I really don't like where this relationship is going. I don't like the way he treats me, and I am no longer happy. I need to make a change, but then I would be alone. What if I don't meet someone for a very long time, or at all for that matter? What if this relationship is the best that I can hope for? Maybe I'm not good enough or don't deserve a better relationship. If I leave him, I will have to change where I live. What if I can't find a good place to live? There are so many unknowns. I don't want to be alone. Maybe I should just suck it up and make the best out of a bad situation. At least I can say that I have someone. Alone I am weak and vulnerable. I better just be grateful for what I have."

So many people succumb to their fear of change and many other subtler manifestations of this fear. They live a life of quiet desperation, as opposed to the unknown outcome of change. We project the worst-case scenario on our future, and we decide not to change. We settle. We give in. We give up.

I hope this has shown you the type of fear we will be addressing. This kind of fear will prevent you from taking that all-important first step toward living your dream. I hope you understand that imagined fear is one of the main obstacles you will overcome on your path to becoming the person you want to become and living the life you want to live. It is my hope that this chapter has increased your awareness and understanding of fear. Fear, being imaginary and unreal, has a hard time standing up to any scrutiny. Like a dark room, it cannot withstand you turning on the light. You will continue to build upon this awareness and understanding as you move through this book.

CHAPTER 2 KEY TAKEAWAYS

- Unless there is a lion, tiger, or bear involved, any fear you experience will almost always be imagined and unreal.
- This psychological fear has affected your life in many ways.
- Psychological fear is one of the biggest obstacles you must overcome.

CHAPTER 3

FOCUSING YOUR POWER TO CHANGE

"The best thing one can do when
it's raining is to let it rain."

~HENRY WADSWORTH LONGFELLOW

In the first two chapters you clarified what you want in your life and what you do not want, developed a burning desire to change, and gained awareness of the types of fear that will hold you back on your journey. You learned and practiced a couple of fundamental NLP techniques you can use to improve the quality of your life in every way.

What I am going to share with you in this chapter has been a beautiful design for living for me. It has afforded me a level of peace and serenity and contentment that is difficult to put into words. It has helped me deal with the speed bumps and roadblocks in my life with a measure of grace and humility. It has helped me deal with life-on-life terms and has helped me to find joy in even the most difficult of circumstances in my life. It has helped me deal with the loss of relationships, family crisis, job changes, economic insecurity, the death of family and friends, illnesses, and countless less calamitous situations like daily interactions with other human beings.

What you will learn in this chapter is how to free up your power to change and to then focus that power on things you can control. We will start by examining the fundamental message found in a very well-known prayer/meditation. If you do not believe in prayer, that's ok. Just take out the God part and make this a meditation. You will achieve the same desired result.

THE SERENITY PRAYER – A PARADIGM SHIFT

**God, grant me the serenity to accept the things
I cannot change,
the courage to change the things I can,
and the wisdom to know the difference.
Living one day at a time.
Enjoying one moment at a time.
Accepting hardship as a pathway to peace.
Taking this sinful world as it is,
not as I would have it.
Knowing that He will make all things right
when I surrender to his will.
That I might be reasonably happy in this life,
and supremely happy in Eternity.**

The message this prayer or meditation is trying to communicate and the paradigm shift it elicits are simple. Understanding this message is a huge step toward your personal freedom. With this understanding we can free ourselves from worry, pain, fear, and stress. We can take all the energy caught up in these emotions and focus it on positive endeavors.

In this chapter we will focus on three key points:

1. **There are things in life I have no control over.**
2. **There are things in life I have control over.**
3. **There is most definitely a difference.**

By accepting and applying these truths, we can find peace in our lives and stop wasting precious time and energy on things outside of our control. We can then focus all our power on things we can control. Let's consider each one separately to gain a better understanding of what is within our control and what is not.

RECLAIMING YOUR POWER TO CHANGE

Acceptance is a skill we can develop. By accepting things we have no control over, we limit the power the external world and external circumstances have over us. We have no direct control over anything in life that is not us. Let me put that in a different way to allow it to sink in. If things are exterior to us, if they are outside of us, not us, if they have already happened, then we have no power to directly control them. Attempting to do so will only cause emotions of fear, stress, anxiety, worry, angst, resentment, regret, and shame, just to name a few. When we make our success, contentment, happiness, self-esteem, and self-worth contingent upon things outside of our control, we set ourselves up for failure and disappointment.

There are three basic categories of things we cannot control. We will take a deeper look into each one and gain a better understanding of what we can and cannot control.

- **People**
- **External Things and Circumstances**
- **The Past**

PEOPLE

Let's take a quick look at some examples of what we can and cannot control when dealing with other people:

I cannot control other people's driving, but I can control how I react to their driving.

I cannot control people's opinion of me, but I can choose to not let that affect my self-confidence or self-worth.

I cannot control how people act toward me and treat me, but I can control how I respond to their actions, what it means to me, and decide whether I should allow it to go any further or set new boundaries.

I cannot control that people's beliefs about the issues of the world may contradict my own beliefs, but I can respect their position as being their position, and not need them to agree with me to feel secure with my own beliefs.

I cannot control how other people live their lives, but I can have compassion for them and be a good role model by becoming the best version of myself I can possibly be.

I cannot control how people act toward each other. I cannot control their violence. I cannot control their hatred. What I can control is my decision to love everyone that I see and everyone that I think about.

No matter what people are doing, I always have it within my power to accept them. To realize that if I had lived all the moments of their life, I might think or behave in a similar fashion. I do not have to like it. I do not have to condone it. I need only accept that they are who they are and accept that I have no power to change them.

No matter what other people are doing, I always have it in my power to love them. To realize that they may be in pain or suffering, that they do not need judgment, but what they need is compassion and forgiveness and love. The nice thing about forgiving others and feeling compassion and love toward them is that I get to feel the feelings of forgiveness, compassion, and love. I benefit from these feelings, even if they do not.

We create problems and turmoil in our lives when we refuse to accept that we cannot change or control others. We develop resentments. We become a victim and allow them to treat us poorly. We believe their opinions of us. We get angry and afraid and spend countless hours of our precious lives caught up in what other people are thinking and doing. We second-guess ourselves and compromise our integrity. When we do, we are giving them power over the quality of our lives. They cannot take this power from us. We must give it to them.

By accepting others, we allow ourselves to focus all our energy and power on improving ourselves and our lives. This may sound selfish to some, to focus all our energy and power on ourselves. Charity and service are some of the best things we can do to evolve and grow, to bring joy and prosperity into our lives. We cannot give away something we do not have though. By focusing our power on improving ourselves and our lives, we are increasing what we can give to others. We are increasing our ability to help others.

EXTERNAL THINGS AND CIRCUMSTANCES

This basically covers everything external to us that is not another human being. I will give a few examples below. Please remember that I am not advocating that you do not care about these things or that you do not help with these things in any way. This is not about burying our heads in the sand. I want you to become acutely aware of the difference between focusing on the problem and focusing on the solution. The problem is what has been and cannot be changed. The solution is what can be, and can definitely be influenced. When we accept that things are what they are, that they have happened or are happening, it allows us to focus our power on the solution and how we can be a part of that solution.

When we complain about something being how it is, or negatively wish something never would have happened, we root ourselves in the problem and give away our power to respond. When we fear all the potential negative implications the situation may hold and the different ways it might affect our lives in a negative way, we are not focusing on what we would like our lives to be like relative to this uncontrollable life situation. Whatever we focus our power on, we strengthen. So, we can focus on the problem and strengthen the problem, or we can focus on the solution and strengthen the solution. Accepting the problem as being what it is allows us to shift our power from problem to solution.

Examples of external circumstances we cannot control are losing a home to a fire, your car breaking down, pandemics, economic downturns, natural disasters, not getting the promotion you worked hard for, getting in a car accident, traffic being horrible, the weather, a missing food item from your take-out order... the list could go on and on.

Some of these things can be devastating, and by no means should we not allow ourselves to experience them. We should by no means keep ourselves from feeling the feelings we need to feel. This would be unhealthy. We need to allow what needs to happen, to happen. Allowance and acceptance are very similar.

We can focus our power on worrying about these things, getting angry about these things, feeling like a victim because of these things, and wishing these things never would have happened, or we can accept that they have happened, allow ourselves to feel what needs to be felt, and focus our power on how we want to and need to respond to these situations.

We can stay caught up in the problem if we would like to. We can brood over it for a day, or a week, or a month. We can resist the idea that it happened for the rest of our lives, but it will not change that it happened. The sooner we accept things we do not want to accept, the sooner we can focus on things we do want.

THE PAST

We will be working on this in greater detail in Chapters 4 and 5, but I wanted to give a brief explanation now. The past does not exist. Let me say that again. The past does not exist. The only place it exists is in our minds. There is nothing we can do to change what has happened, to make something unhappen. We cannot change what we have believed, thought, felt, or how we have acted. We cannot change what other people have done. We can change nothing that has happened in this universe up to this moment.

You can add your current situation to this as well. Where you are at in this moment results directly from your past beliefs, thoughts, emotions, actions, reactions, and intentions. We see things as they were in the past. When we see the light from the sun, we are seeing the sun as it was eight minutes ago because it takes eight minutes for the light from the sun to reach our eyes. The same is true for every physical object we see. We see these objects as they were, not as they are. We will not be going into quantum physics and how our consciousness influences matter; that is for another book. I want you to let this distinction settle in:

We cannot change anything that already is. We can only work to influence that which will be.

As we will find out in Chapters 4 and 5, what we can change is what our past means to us, and we can change the value of all the moments of our past by learning the lessons they were meant to teach us, squeezing all the wisdom we can out of these moments.

FOCUSING YOUR POWER TO CHANGE

It was difficult for me to accept some of the truths discussed in the previous section. I think I felt that if I accepted that something happened, that somehow I was saying it was ok. What I learned is that if I stop putting my energy into fighting what has been and what needs to change, that I could focus all my energy on being the change that is needed.

This leads me to just focusing the power to change on things we can control so we can become a better person, live a better life, and make this a better world to live in. We have gone over the fact that who we are and the life we are living results directly from our beliefs, thoughts, emotions, actions, reactions, and intentions up to this point. We have gone over the fact that we are the cause, and our lives are the effect. We have also gone over the definition of insanity as doing the same things over and over and expecting different results. What I am getting at is that if we want a higher quality of life, then we must develop a higher quality of beliefs, thoughts, emotions, actions, responses, and intentions for our life. Lucky for us, this is completely within our power to control.

Let's take a brief look at each one of these factors and how we can directly control them. In the following chapters, we will learn specific techniques to change these things and take action to do so.

INTENTIONS

We cover living your life with intention in greater detail in Part 2. What you intend your life to look like is completely up to you. We have the power to choose how we will live our lives. Unfortunately, so many of us never claim this power. So many of us are just ok taking what life gives us. There is something to be said for "living life on life's terms," as we cannot always control the exact form our intentions will manifest in our lives or know the exact method by which they will be manifested. We must be willing to continue to grow and evolve, and as we continue to grow and evolve, our intentions will grow and evolve. You can take what life gives you by default, or you can design the life you want to live and become the person you need to become in order to live that life. This is completely within your control.

BELIEFS

Our beliefs control how we subjectively experience our objective reality, resulting in our thoughts, emotions, actions, and reactions in relation to this subjective reality. We respond to our beliefs about reality and not to reality itself. Here is an example of how beliefs can change our subjective experience of reality:

The president of the company has called a meeting to go over the quarterly numbers. The company did not meet projections in many key departments, including your own. The president goes over the numbers and also shares key insights and suggestions and speaks to the current state of the industry. She asks everyone to redouble their efforts and raises the projections for next quarter.

Now depending on what I believe to be true, I can experience this in several ways. For example, if I believe I am good at my job and always provide quality work, and believe in my ability to continue to grow, I might believe the following to be true about the meeting:

"We didn't end up where we wanted to as a team. I see some key areas that I can work on as well as some areas I can improve on that will help quite a few different departments. This could be the opportunity to shine that I have been looking for. We have a great president who knows her stuff and she wouldn't set a projection that she didn't believe we could hit. Sounds like it's going to be a good quarter. Maybe I'll hit that bonus I've been trying so hard for."

Now if I believed the opposite, then I might believe something different.

"She looks frustrated. I think I may be in trouble here, but it also looks like there are quite a few department heads in trouble. That's good. She can't fire all of us. They better not throw me under the bus. She wants us to try all these different things. When was the last time she did my job? She wouldn't last a second in my department. We are doing the best we can. And the projections for next quarter are too high. We didn't hit last quarter's numbers and she is going to increase them?! That's crazy. She is totally setting us up for failure. I wonder if she's doing that on purpose so she can find a reason to fire me."

Now, this is an extremely basic example, but hopefully, it helps you understand beliefs a little better. You can take the exact same objective input, and depending on what you believe, your perception of what is "true" about this situation will be different. There are no "right" or "wrong" beliefs. It's just a matter of if they are serving us the way we would like them to.

So, our beliefs influence our thoughts about any situation. Our thoughts influence our emotions, which influence our actions, which bring about our circumstances. Our beliefs, no matter how close to the truth they are, are like self-fulfilling prophecies. In later chapters, you will learn to identify your beliefs and make sure that what you believe aligns with who you want to become and the life you want to live.

THOUGHTS

Our thoughts are formed based upon the information that made it through the filters of our beliefs. As illustrated in the previous section, our thoughts will vary depending on the belief. Our thoughts will show us what we believe to be true, even if we have no conscious awareness of that belief.

By learning the techniques and completing the exercises in this book, your awareness of your thoughts will grow by leaps and bounds. You will develop the ability to put a PAUSE between stimulus and response. This will allow you time to decide whether this thought is true for you or not, to measure this thought against your current values and future ideals. If they do not measure up, you will develop the ability to stop the thought right there and not act upon it. You will also learn to trace that thought back to the belief that caused it. Chances are, if the thought does not match up to your values and ideals, then the belief that created it does not match up either. You have the ability to control and change your thoughts.

EMOTIONS

Our emotions are a reaction or response to a thought, either conscious or subconscious. Some emotional responses can be lightning-fast and happen before we have a chance to consider them. This is called a reaction. We react to a situation rather than examining it and then intentionally responding to it. Reactions can be a good thing. Especially if they are keeping you alive and safe from real danger. They are not a good thing when creating unneeded negative consequences in your life.

To emotionally respond to a situation or execute a designed reaction is a different thing altogether. The best way to control your emotions is to control your thoughts. To insert a PAUSE between thought and emotion. Once an emotion gets going, wanted or unwanted, it gets harder to change. You will learn how to intentionally and deliberately design how you would like to react and respond to any life situation. You need not be a slave to past programmed emotional responses. You can control and change how you feel about any situation.

ACTIONS

By this point, the cause of any action you make has gone through quite a few stages. You had a belief about a situation, which created some thoughts about the situation; you then had an emotional response to these thoughts, which moved you to the point where you took action, or in some cases, chose not to act.

There is no reason we cannot take full responsibility for our actions especially after reading this book in which you will learn how to be intentional about your beliefs, thoughts, and emotions. It is when we take action that we create the circumstances of our lives. We can believe in something, think about it, and get all worked up and emotionally charged about it, but nothing will happen, good or bad, until we act.

When we think about actions, we usually think about going out and making things happen. And this is indeed an example of taking action. One equally important, if not more important, kind of action is the action of communicating with others. The saying "nothing pays off like restraint in tongue and pen" is so true and so important to understand. Once we hit SEND on that email, text, or social media reply, or open our mouths and share with the world exactly how we feel, there is no going back. It's out there. We cannot unring that bell.

We may believe how we see the world is the right way to see it, gather up all our thoughts that support that we are right, and get all fired up and motivated to do something about it, yet we can always stop it right there and decide to not act. Whether or not this action will have positive or negative consequences, we can always choose not to take any action. We can pause and reflect and postpone our actions. We can write down all our options on a piece of paper and we can sleep on it. We can ask the opinion of a close friend or advisor. We have so many choices we can make, which do not include taking action. Discretion is sometimes the better part of valor. All actions you take are completely within your ability to control.

I have presented you with a lot of things to consider. I have challenged you to see life a little differently. Remember, if you do not change, your life will not change. What I would like you to take away from this chapter is an understanding that the answers and the power to change you have been seeking do not exist "out there" somewhere. All the power you will ever need to become the person you want to become and live the life you want to live can be found in only one place, and that is within you.

This whole book is meant to take your attention from the outside and turn it to the inside. You have always had all the power you need; now it is just a matter of finding, refining, and applying it.

INTRODUCTION TO ANCHORS
Anchors are a fundamental technique that utilizes the science of the conditioned response to intentionally program responses we can access at any time we see the value for it. Key things we can include in an anchor are mindsets, beliefs, emotional responses, and self-talk.

The study of conditioned response was made popular by Pavlov's dog experiment. In the 1890s scientist Ivan Pavlov was doing a study on conditioned responses of dogs. He set up an experiment where he would measure the dog's salivation response to food being placed in front of them. He then rang a bell every time he placed food in front of the dogs, allowing the dogs to associate bell ringing and food. He then elicited the same salivary response to the bell without the food. He would ring the bell and the dogs would salivate. This is considered a conditioned response, an automatic reaction to a given stimulus.

A key thing to understand about conditioned responses and anchors is Hebb's law, often summarized as "Cells that fire together, wire together." This means that when nerve cells fire together, a connection is made. When we use this connection again, it is strengthened. Creating an anchor is a very simple process, but creating an anchor you can use at will over time that is powerful and automatic takes practice. There is power in repetition, repetition, repetition.

EXERCISE: CREATING AN ACCEPTANCE ANCHOR
The anchor you will create today will allow you to access a feeling of acceptance and surrender (letting go). This is one I use with great success any time I catch myself getting wrapped up in things I cannot control. It works to free me from the line of thinking that has me caught up in an uncontrollable situation. As you continue to use this anchor, your ability to pause your thinking naturally and automatically in uncontrollable situations will increase. You will be programming your mind to be mindful. Your ability to distinguish between things you can and cannot control will grow stronger and stronger. You will also develop your ability to design responses you can use to increase the quality of your life. This is another game-changing skill.

In Chapter 1, you learned about the modalities and submodalities which structure your memories, primarily the visual, auditory, and kinesthetic components. You can create an anchor based upon just one of these, but the effectiveness will be greatly increased by bringing into the anchor all three in as much detail as possible.

There are many types of anchors. In Pavlov's experiment, when the dog saw the food and salivated, the image of the food was a visual anchor. When the dog heard the bell and salivated, the sound of the bell was an auditory anchor. Any trigger that elicits a specific response can be considered an anchor. What we will be creating is called a kinesthetic anchor or physical anchor. This anchor will be the stimulus for your intended conditioned response. What you will need to do is find a place on your body where you want to set the anchor. I like to touch my thumb to a particular knuckle. I have a three-by-five card with an index of what is anchored to each knuckle. After you have set this anchor successfully, you can access the state of acceptance by simply touching this area as you did when you set it, or what we call "firing the anchor."

Once you have chosen the place to set the anchor, you will need to create the response you'd like to anchor, so in this case, acceptance. What I'd like to do is have you search your mind for memories where you were in a state of acceptance or letting go. A moment where you realized there was nothing you could do, and with this realization you found a measure of peace or closure. If you cannot find a memory you can just imagine one. The mind does not know the difference, but it is always easier if you can access an actual memory.

When you have it, step into that memory as if it was happening right now. See what you saw in as much detail as possible, remember any sounds or anything you were saying to yourself, and especially important is to feel how you felt, both physical sensations and emotions. Pay close attention to how you are breathing and your body posture. Write down as many details as possible about the structure of that memory using the submodality list below.

- **Visual-** Location of image, size, is it framed like a TV or panoramic, black and white or color, moving or still, associated (seeing through your eyes) or dissociated (seeing as if a neutral observer)
- **Auditory-** Volume, Speed, Location, Tonality
- **Kinesthetic-** Location of feeling, shape, movement, pressure, color

Once you have your list, set it aside and break your state. Do some jumping jacks. Imagine and say your phone number backwards. Look at a few things in the room and remember where you got them. A break state is like a palate cleanse. This is very important.

Now I would like you to go back to the beginning of this chapter and memorize The Serenity Prayer/Meditation and create an image of it in your mind. We will be adding auditory and visual content to the anchor.

Following this process is very important.

Reimagine the moment of acceptance you wrote down. Bring in all the VAK of the experience and make it as real as possible.

Match your breathing and posture.

Once you are there, bring the image of the Serenity Prayer into mind and speak it out loud. Each time you say it, imagine that the feeling of acceptance, of peace, of surrender is increasing in every way. Feel it build up in your body and enter every cell of your being. You can play with submodalities as well, as we discussed in Chapter 1. Make things brighter or larger or louder, etc. Whatever you can do to increase the intensity and power of the experience, do it.

Now this is the key. When your experience is at its peak is when you are going to set the anchor. Hold the anchor as long as the experience is at its peak, and when it diminishes, simply let go.

This is the process for setting an anchor. This is your first time doing this, so be patient with yourself. Your ability to do this will increase with time, and as your ability to do this increases so will the power of the anchors. Take a deep breath. Get comfortable. Go over the steps in your mind. Now set your anchor.

Let's check and see how that anchor took. Break your state as you did before. Now fire the anchor again. Each person will experience this differently. Do not be discouraged if firing the anchor this first time doesn't take you back 100% to the state you created. You will be strengthening this anchor through repetition and intensity. Go through this process at least five more times. The more, the better. The process will be:

- Fire your anchor.
- Increase the intensity of the state.
- At its peak, fire the anchor again and hold it until it diminishes.
- Break state.

I reinforce my major anchors daily as a part of my success program and use the anchors at appropriate times throughout my day.

WHEN TO USE YOUR ANCHOR

A word on expectations: This will not work perfectly, as nothing in this universe works perfectly. The results will vary depending on the intensity of the situation and the strength of the anchor. Think of this as an averaging out of energy. Unwanted state + positive anchor = new state. The more you use this anchor the stronger it will become. I use my acceptance anchor any time I think about something I cannot control or when I become emotionally involved in something I cannot control. The longer you wait to use this, the less effective it becomes. For instance, it would be less effective to fire your anchor if you have been angry about something and have been brooding over it for a long time and are now thinking about acting on it. The earlier in the cause-and-effect chain you fire it, the more effective it will be.

Whenever you feel like you are caught up in something you cannot change having a hard time accepting something, or have something that you really want to let go of, fire your anchor and say the Serenity Prayer. Speaking the words out loud is the most powerful way of practicing it, but saying it to yourself works as well. Say the Serenity Prayer as many times as you need to until you drive the unwanted thoughts or feelings out of your mind, and then move on with your day. If the unwanted thought or feeling comes up again, as soon as you recognize it, repeat this process.

Once you get comfortable with this process, you can design a whole set of anchors. Remember Hebb's law; cells that fire together wire together. It's all about repetition and intensity. This is a technique that must be learned and practiced and strengthened. This is a technique that, when mastered, will allow you to make massive changes in yourself and in your life.

What you have learned in this chapter, when practiced and applied to your life, will increase the quality of every area of your life. You are now equipped with a tool that will allow you to consciously and deliberately respond to any given situation or trigger. The better you get at focusing your power on things you can control, the faster you will be able to create the changes in your life you are looking for.

CHAPTER 3 KEY TAKEAWAYS

- We cannot control people, places, things, or the past.
- We can control everything about ourselves.
- By accepting things outside of our control, we can focus all our power on becoming the person we want to become and living the life we want to live.
- By creating an anchor, we can create intentional conditioned responses we can use in any situation we perceive as being advantageous.
- By mastering the skill of anchoring, we can truly live our life intentionally and deliberately. We will no longer be slaves to our unwanted reactions to life.

CHAPTER 4

THE PERSONAL INVENTORY

"Let there be nothing within thee that is not very beautiful and very gentle, and there will be nothing without thee that is not beautiful and softened by the spell of thy presence."

~ JAMES ALLEN

The things you will learn about yourself and the steps you will take in this chapter will change you and your life forever. The process I will walk you through will allow you to look at all the ways fear has manifested in your life. By completing your Personal Inventory, you will see how events from your past are still causing pain and difficulties and holding you back in your life. You will see how your power, call it your spirit or soul, is still caught up in the past. By doing a thorough and fearless Personal Inventory, you will begin freeing yourself and your power from your past.

THE PERSONAL INVENTORY

So what are we taking inventory of? We will be looking at all the fears you currently know. We will also look at resentments and regrets, acts of harm both committed by you and against you, and we will look at intimate relationships in your life to uncover some fears you may not be aware of. We will be focused only on things within your control and will be focused only on your part in it. We will be looking for patterns of thinking, feeling, and behaving that are holding you back and causing you pain. This will be one of the most rewarding things you have ever done in your life. The lasting positive changes it produces will be directly proportional to how honest and thorough you are with this inventory.

The first time I did this inventory I came up with 49 things that caused me pain in the past. Things like insecurities in relationships and how they manifested themselves to the detriment of everyone involved. Things like being dishonest to mask my low self-esteem and fear of failure. There was the regret and shame I had for all the times I treated my mother and father poorly, and the things I put them through. There was the regret, shame, and pain I held about the times I acted in a less than loving way toward my children and wife. There were the resentments I had and beliefs I had adopted from those that hurt me physically in my life. There were the laws I had broken that resulted from my wanting to fit in and wanting to be accepted. There was my judgment of others and my gossiping about others, all stemming from not feeling like I was good enough. Basically, everything I had done up to that point in my life that was not up to the standards of how I wanted to live.

The most important thing I got out of this inventory was finding out what the cause of all my pain and suffering and unwanted behavior has been. When I traced back all these items to the cause of them and what my part in it was, I was shocked to see they all traced back to one form of fear or another: Fear I wouldn't get something I thought I couldn't live without, or fear of losing something that I thought I needed to be happy, secure, and safe. Some fears I came up with on my first inventory were the fear of being alone, the fear of rejection, the fear of not being in control, the fear of not being good enough, the fear of change, the fear that my body wasn't good enough, the fear of mentally ill people, the fear of homeless people, the fear of failure, the fear of public speaking, the fear of confrontation, the fear of disease, the fear of not being perfect, the fear of being responsible and letting people down, the fear of suffering a loss, the fear of poverty, the fear of losing my job, the fear of failing as a father and husband, and the fear of losing my spouse. I traced all these fears back to threats to my three basic instincts: Survival, sex, and social. Instincts are very simple, very old programs meant to keep us alive and keep the species moving forward.

Instinct Examples:

- **Survival Instinct:** I don't want to die.
- **Sex Instinct:** I want to have babies.
- **Social Instinct:** I don't want to get kicked out of the tribe. If I do, I won't be able to have babies and the lions, tigers, and bears will eat me.

These instinctual fears, until I did something about them, were in the background, affecting every area of my life. I share these very personal things with you because I sincerely want you to get the most out of this inventory that you can. I share these things with you because this was the most important thing I have ever done to grow as a person and increase the quality of my life. I share these things with you because, even though we have never met, I can honestly say I love you, and the only reason I can honestly say that is because I did this inventory. I share these things with you so you can see how deep this can go and to give you the courage to dig as deep as you can. It may sound like I am overselling this, but I am not. If you do only one exercise, do this one.

Maybe you don't have a lot to put on your inventory, which is great. As a human, though, I know there is something that you are holding on to that is no longer serving you, something that you can let go of and free yourself from. No human is perfect or will ever be perfect. I have done two more inventories like this since the first time. Each time I have found subtler manifestations of fear acting on my life. There will always be growth available if I seek it. I humbly ask you to search your personal history with all the honesty, open-mindedness, and willingness you can muster.

THE PERSONAL INVENTORY
We will break this inventory up into four parts: Resentments and Regrets, Harms, Romantic Relationships, and Fears. I put fears last because in each of the three preceding parts you will uncover fears you may not have known that you had. At the end of this chapter, I have provided four blank worksheets, although you may need to make copies if needed. I know I did.

PART 1: RESENTMENTS AND REGRETS
They say that harboring a resentment is like drinking poison and expecting the other person to get sick. Common manifestations of resentments are grudges, negative opinions, bitterness, anger, irritation, hostility. It is not only people we resent but also anything that we feel these feelings towards.

We can also hold resentments toward whole groups of people, governments, religions, companies, organizations, and all the ideas and beliefs that accompany them. The only person we harm by harboring resentment is ourselves.

Regret is simply a resentment toward oneself. This can also manifest as shame and guilt, which can turn into all types of self-loathing and self-hatred, and any other pain we choose to inflict upon ourselves. When we think things like "I wish I would have" or "I shouldn't have done that" or "I am bad because I did this" or "I am not good enough because I did this," we are not forgiving ourselves and are thus holding resentments toward ourselves. Every time we indulge ourselves in regret, we hurt our self-esteem.

By learning to let go of resentments and regrets and learning to forgive ourselves and all those involved, we can heal ourselves and stop inflicting unneeded and unhelpful pain against ourselves. We will cover how to do this in greater detail in Chapter 5.

Now it's time for your inventory. You will notice that the resentments and regrets worksheet has five columns: Who you resent; Why you resent them; What instincts were threatened; What our part in it was; and the Ideal. Start by listing every resentment and regret you have in column one. Be as thorough as you can with this. If you think you have resentment, but are not 100% sure, write it down anyway. Further investigation will reveal the truth about it. Once you have completed column one, take each resentment through the next four columns. When you have completed one resentment, then move on to the next resentment.

WHO YOU RESENT

Again, anyone you are angry at, including yourself. Also pay close attention to any time anyone has hurt or harmed you emotionally, mentally, physically, financially, or socially. There may be resentment hiding there.

WHY YOU RESENT THEM

For instance, someone is angry with their co worker Steve because he stole their idea for the new process and took credit for it.

WHAT INSTINCTS WERE THREATENED

In the above example, it would probably be social, as it takes away an opportunity to improve their standing at work. Although, it could be the other two if it may lead to their spouse leaving them or threaten their ability to pay their bills.

WHAT WAS OUR PART IN IT

This is the most important part. Ask yourself, with an honest and open mind, "Was there anything that I did, or didn't do, that caused or allowed this to happen?" Maybe, in the above example, the person had many opportunities to share their ideas, only they didn't because of their fears of failure and not being good enough. Maybe they stole the idea from someone else. Maybe they were gossiping about Steve, and Steve found out about it and the stealing of their idea was meant as revenge. If we look close enough, we can usually find some level of responsibility for the situation. This does not mean you need to make something up or take credit for someone else doing you wrong. We cannot control them. All we can do is get as much good out of the situation as we can. Just be as honest and open-minded and objective as you can.

There will be certain things we do not have a part in and hold no responsibility for. For instance, I was sexually assaulted by an adult when I was twelve years old and molested by my babysitter when I was ten. I had no part in these. Please, if you have been assaulted in any way, do not own that. It was not your fault, and it was not ok. In Chapter 5, I will share with you how I was able to come to accept that this happened to me, and how I forgave them.

THE IDEAL
Now, looking at the first four columns, ask yourself how you would like to respond if it happens again. If there is anything in column four, ask yourself what you could have done differently. If you see any behaviors or character traits you do not like, what would be the desired behavior or trait you would like to replace that with?

When you have completed this process with all your resentments, you will have come up with a lot of things to consider. Are there any patterns? Is one instinct threatened more than the others? Are there patterns of behavior you see in column four? How about column five; are there any recurring themes going on there?

Before you move on to the next part, stop and allow yourself to feel good about what you have done so far. It takes courage and strength to do what you have done. You have done something that most people are unwilling to do. You have taken a huge step that will increase the quality of your life.

PART 2: HARMS
In this part, you will search your past and learn how you have harmed others: Things like verbally abusing them, gossiping

about them, stealing from them, assaulting them, damaging their property, making up lies about them, and basically anything we have done selfishly that has hurt someone emotionally, mentally, physically, financially, or socially. If people are directly harmed by your choice to not do something, you can also put that down.

You can put down anything that you have done to harm yourself as well. It could be anything that you had a regret about in Part 1. It could be something like drinking alcohol, smoking, doing drugs, or eating foods we know aren't healthy for us. It could be any self-destructive behavior you are aware of.

The Harms worksheet provided is broken up into four columns: Who was harmed, How they were harmed, Why I harmed them, and The Ideal. As in the resentment inventory, you will complete column one first, then go back to each harm and work through all the columns. Then move on to the next one.

WHO WAS HARMED
Again, everyone, including yourself, who was hurt in any way.

HOW THEY WERE HARMED
Were they hurt physically, mentally, emotionally, financially, or socially?

WHY I HARMED THEM
Take your time on this one. Bring yourself back to the moment these harms occurred and ask yourself why you harmed them. Really relive the moment as you did before in previous exercises. See what you saw. Hear what you heard. Feel what you felt. Think what you thought. What you are looking for is the

emotion and thoughts and beliefs that led up to harming someone. What was your true motivation? If you cannot find a definite why, leave the column blank for now. More is always being revealed.

For instance, I committed a crime when I was younger because I wanted to fit in. I felt peer pressure, and I was afraid that I would not fit in if I didn't do the crime. This is an example of my social instinct being threatened. Had I done it to pay my bills then it would be the survival instinct. Had I done it to impress a girl, then it would have been the sex instinct.

THE IDEAL

Looking at this worksheet again, ask yourself, "If I could do it all over again, what would I do differently?" If you see any behaviors or character traits you do not like, what would be the desired behavior or trait you would like to replace it with?

Before you move on to Part 3, take a little time to let things sink in for you. Reflect upon it. What are your key takeaways from this inventory so far? Has this inventory created an awareness of some of your growth opportunities? When I was at this point, I was getting pretty down on myself. Then I was reminded that I cannot change what I have done and cannot change something if I do not know it is there. I was reminded that I was taking the steps necessary to make things right and make sure I didn't do these things again. I was doing what most people would not be willing to do. Please know this is not the time for morbid reflection or beating yourself up. This is a time to celebrate your willingness to change and the courage you have exhibited so far.

PART 3: ROMANTIC RELATIONSHIPS

This is not a book on relationships, although this book will improve how you show up in every relationship moving forward. There will be no advice given or relationship strategies shared. This is a book on how to change ourselves and change our lives. The world is our mirror. It reflects what is going on in our inner world. Romantic relationships are more like magnifying glasses than mirrors. They show us the stuff deep down inside of us, things we may not consciously be aware of. The purpose of this inventory is to become aware of any fears, beliefs, unwanted character traits, and unwanted behaviors that our romantic relationships may have revealed to us.

Now, if you can honestly say you have never had problems in a romantic relationship, then skip this one. If you have had relationship issues in the past, though, then Part 3 will shine a lot of light on what has been causing you troubles, and by learning their causes, you will be in a position where you can remedy them.

In this inventory, you will be looking at how you have contributed to the pain and unhappiness of your partner and yourself in current and past relationships. Things that may make this list are acts of jealousy, insecurity of any kind, attempts at control, verbal abuse, physical abuse, or emotional or sexual infidelity. Write down anything you have ever done in any relationship you feel guilty or ashamed of. If you have stayed in bad relationships longer than you should have, write that down. If you always get into relationships with the wrong type of person, write that down. If you discover any unwanted relationship trends that have caused you or your partner pain, write those down.

The Romantic Relationship worksheet has been broken up into five columns: Relationship, What happened, My Part in it, Was I ever, and The Ideal. You will complete this worksheet as you did the first two.

RELATIONSHIP
Write down every romantic relationship in which there were any troubles. If your problem is not enough romantic relationships, write that down too.

WHAT HAPPENED
This can be anything that you had a part in that harmed either of you physically, mentally, emotionally, financially, or socially. What were the common points of contention? What did you fight about most often? Were there any events that happened of note? When you were worried or afraid in this relationship, what is it you feared? Write down anything you can think of that you are ashamed of or feel guilty about.

MY PART IN IT
This is where you write down how you contributed to the situation. Look at the seven options in the next column. Did any of these cause you to act in a way you did not want to? Write down anything you feel you should write down.

WAS I EVER?
There are seven common unresourceful behaviors/character traits listed here. If you think of any you feel are not there, simply write them in.

- **Jealousy**
- **Insecurity**

- **Controlling behavior (needing to control the person's activities, feelings, telling them how they need to behave, etc.)**
- **Being needy (making your happiness dependent upon the love or attention they are giving you)**
- **Being emotionally or physically unfaithful**
- **Being dishonest**
- **Being emotionally, verbally, or physically abusive.**

These seven behaviors/character traits point to fundamental issues within us and will typically manifest themselves in a variety of ways in our lives, not just in our relationships.

THE IDEAL

Looking back at these relationships, ask yourself, "What lessons have I learned that I can bring into my current relationship or my next relationship? Are there any unwanted recurring themes or patterns of behavior? What would I do differently next time? How have I grown? How do I want to think, feel, and act in a relationship?" This is your ideal.

If you have come this far, you have come farther than most. You have looked at your past from quite a few perspectives. You have gotten rigorously honest with yourself about where your opportunities for change and growth are. You have gained a great deal of insight and awareness into who you are and how fear has affected you in your life.

PART 4: FEARS

You have seen throughout this process how fear can manifest in a variety of ways. The purpose of the Fears worksheet is to allow you to name those fears and list whether they are real or imagined. By putting our fears down on paper, we see the truth about them, and they somehow lose a little of their power over us. We see how no fears have ended up in our death. We see that most things we have feared have never happened, and if they did, we will see that we had a part in making that fear a reality.

The Fears worksheet is broken up into five columns: Fear, Real or Imagined, Did it happen, Why do I have it, and The Ideal.

FEAR

Write down every fear that is readily apparent. Every fear you know you have. Here is a hint. Every time you listed an instinct that was threatened on the previous worksheets, there was a fear involved. Some forms of fear that are often overlooked are the fear of failure, the fear of rejection, the fear of abandonment, the fear of not being good enough, and the fear of someone else's negative opinion of you. Write down any phobias as well.

REAL OR IMAGINED

Ask yourself, "Is the fear a reaction to an actual threat to my survival that I am facing right now at this moment?" or "Is this fear a reaction to an imagined situation or outcome that might happen at some point in the future?" If a bear is chasing you, then this fear is real and quite helpful. If a bear is not chasing you, then this fear is imagined and a choice.

DID IT HAPPEN?

Ask yourself, "Did this fear that I have actually become a reality?" and "Did it happen?" If it did happen, ask yourself, "Was this a self-fulfilling prophecy?" meaning, did you consciously or subconsciously contribute to this fear becoming a reality.

WHY DO I HAVE THIS FEAR?
This is your opportunity to get to the cause of your fear. What is the supporting evidence for this fear? Has the thing you fear actually happened before in your life? Is this your fear or did you adopt this fear from someone in your family or community? Allow yourself the time to ask the questions and have the patience to wait for the answers that will come. The reasons we have these fears can be buried deep down some very interesting rabbit holes. Do not be surprised if you get nothing on your first pass. More will always be revealed.

Before you are done with Part 4, look at the Fears worksheet you have in front of you. Take a few deep breaths and get into a peaceful mental state. If it helps you can fire your acceptance anchor. Once you are in a peaceful state, ask these three questions.

- How has this inventory changed how I feel about fear?
- How will this new perspective on fear change my life moving forward?
- Have any of the things I have ever feared in my life actually killed me?

The first time I finished this inventory, I felt numb. There was so much I had brought to the surface that I couldn't consciously process it all. In the following days, events and feelings and understanding kept coming to the surface. My mind was finding new patterns in behaviors and seeing how those affected my life on an even broader scale. This will happen to you as well. More is going to be revealed.

I would like you to take this inventory out and look at it every day for the next few days. Before you begin, ask yourself, "What else can I see here? What did I miss? What lessons and wisdom are here for me?" Invariably things will come up that you left off your first draft. Add them to the appropriate worksheet.

CHAPTER 4 KEY TAKEAWAYS

- Our power and energy are trapped in the unresolved events of our past.
- These unresolved events are experienced as resentments, regrets, and guilt.
- These produce the negative emotions we deal with daily.
- By increasing your awareness of these unresolved events, you can free yourself from them.

RESENTMENTS AND REGRETS WORKSHEET

Who I Resent	Why I Resent Them	Instincts Threatened			My part in it	The Ideal
		Survival	Sex	Social		

HARMS WORKSHEET

Who was harmed	How were they harmed	Why I harmed them	The Ideal

ROMANTIC RELATIONSHIPS WORKSHEET

Relationship	What happened	My Part in it	Was I Ever							The Ideal
			Jealous	Insecure	Controlling	Needy	Unfaithful	Dishonest	Abusive	

Copyright © 2021 by Kyle C. Becker
www.kylecbecker.com

THE PERSONAL INVENTORY

FEAR WORKSHEET

Fear	Real or Imagined?	Did it actually happen?	The Ideal

CHAPTER 5

PART 1: THE FREEDOM TO CHANGE

"We must develop the capacity to forgive.
He who is devoid of the power to forgive is devoid of the power to love."

~ MARTIN LUTHER KING JR.

So far you have made a fearless and thorough inventory of your past fears, beliefs, thoughts, emotions, actions, and reactions and learned how these have affected your life so far. To create positive momentum in our lives, we must free ourselves from all the entanglements holding our power and focus in the past. We must first take care of any negative momentum that is still holding us back. We need to stop doing the things in our lives causing unwanted results in our lives. We have discussed that our life up to this point has resulted from our beliefs, thoughts, emotions, actions, reactions, and intentions (or lack of intention). I like to call this a cause-and-effect chain, or outcome chain. We know that if we continue to do the same things we have always done, we will continue to get the same results we have always gotten. We must learn to break the outcome chains creating the wrong results in our lives. When we break these chains, we will finally be free to change ourselves and our lives. In this chapter we will be focused on doing just that.

I would like to share a metaphor I think will help you see what you have done in Chapter 4 and will continue to do in Chapter 5.

THE CRUCIBLE

A crucible is a metal or earthen container used to subject metals to intense heat and pressure to purify them. When heating metals in a crucible, what you will see happen is the "dross" or impurities will come to the top, allowing you to skim them off. That is what you have done in Chapter 4. You have created a crucible and subjected your life to the heat of your awareness to begin the process of purification. In Chapter 5, you will turn up the heat a bit by adding a little pressure to it. You will then begin removing the impurities. You will break the chain of any past beliefs, thoughts, emotions, or behaviors causing you trouble. You will free your mind from the pain and failures of the past so you can wholeheartedly turn your attention to the future.

LAY DOWN YOUR BURDENS

The first step in being forgiven and forgiving ourselves is to confess our shortcomings by reading our Personal Inventory aloud to another human being. We need to get it out of our heads and hear and see it objectively. Think of it as a form of confession.

I would like to share with you the experience I had the first time I read my inventory to another human being. I ended up reading my inventory to my father and my AA sponsor. The process I am sharing with you now was inspired by the process AA has used successfully to help countless alcoholics and addicts free themselves from the wreckage of their past and help them lay a solid foundation to build a new and better life upon. It is almost a magical process, as the results that people receive are downright magical.

As I mentioned in the previous chapter, my inventory consisted of forty-nine items. Each item included four to five columns. So roughly 200 to 250 things I read to my sponsor and father. It was very thorough and honest. I left nothing off of it I was aware of at the time.

I read my inventory to my sponsor line by line, baring my soul to him and leaving nothing out. Sometimes, I felt resistance when I came up to an item that felt especially embarrassing or shameful, but powered through any resistance I felt. I was determined to read everything I had on my inventory. I didn't want any of it anymore. I was ready to lay down my burdens. I was ready to forgive and be forgiven. I told him things I had told no one in my entire life. Secrets that had burdened me for decades. The biggest mistakes of my life. Resentments. Crimes I had committed. People I had hurt. People I had let down. Fears. Shame. Regret. Things I thought I could never forgive. I couldn't believe the things coming out of my mouth, the things I was sharing with another human being. There were things I felt compelled to read with my father. I finished reading my inventory with him. It was a moment I believe both of us will remember for the rest of our lives.

While reading my inventory, I experienced some of my hurts and pains and shame being immediately taken from me. Getting them off my chest and out of my mind and shining the light of reality on them, I gained freedom from them. The healing tears of joy wet my face as the weight of them was lifted from me. Just speaking them aloud released all the power they held over me. As I continued to read, the energy that built up in me, and was flowing through me, was palpable. It had a dense, heavy feeling to it and, at the same time, felt expansive and light. At times I was overwhelmed, but I powered through. When I was finished, I felt absolutely numb. The energy flowing through me was more than I could process.

When I was done reading my inventory, I found a quiet place to reflect upon what I had just done. It was just me and my God. As I sat in quiet contemplation, wonderful things happened. Growing within me was a profound willingness to change whatever needed to be changed. To let go of whatever needed to be let go of. I felt character traits and beliefs that had caused me pain loosen their grip on me. I felt like I had purged so much negative energy that it had left holes in the psychological and emotional structure of my being. It was like I was sitting in a house and suddenly, a whole wall was missing, letting the light pour in. It was one of the most powerful and transformative moments of my life.

In completing your Personal Inventory, you have no doubt brought to the surface emotions and fears and pain you had buried deep within yourself. You have begun to recognize how your unwanted beliefs, thinking, emotions, behaviors, reactions, and fears have affected the quality of your life and the lives of those around you. You have identified resentments you may have against others or yourself and you have identified any guilt, remorse, or shame you have for the things you have done to yourself and others. More work must be done to free yourself from these feelings. By freeing ourselves from these feelings, we can free ourselves from the outcome chains that created these feelings. If we do not work toward freeing ourselves, by forgiving or being forgiven, our old way of thinking will continue, as will the results in our lives associated with them.

You may have been carrying around these burdens, these resentments, regrets, and pain for a long time. They have weighed you down like an anchor, impeding your progress. You have shouldered these burdens long enough. You don't have to carry them any longer. By reading your inventory to another human being, you begin to lay down your burdens.

Choosing the right person to read your inventory to is particularly important. You want to make sure that the person you choose will not be hurt by anything you will reveal in your inventory. You will want to choose someone you trust to confide in. This can be a trusted friend, parent, brother or sister, a spiritual advisor (priest, reverend, rabbi), doctor, or therapist. After choosing the right person and securing their willingness to listen to your inventory, the only thing left to do is read it to them.

If there is absolutely no one in your life that you can read it to (not having anyone available and not being willing to read it to anyone are two different things), read it out loud to your God. If you don't believe in a power greater than yourself, then read it to the forest or to the ocean. Get it out of your mind though. Speak it. Reveal it to the light of awareness of all that is. Get creative if you must, but read it. You will be so grateful that you did. It really is an awesome feeling, and the results in your state of being will amaze you.

Depending on the size of your inventory, this process should take an hour or so. When I listen to someone's inventory, I like to stay silent the whole time unless they specifically ask me for my guidance. I like to allow their energy to build up in them as much as possible. You may want to instruct the person listening to your inventory to do the same. Ultimately, if you are honest and thorough and courageous in this, it will work itself out exactly as it was meant to be.

You will be reading your inventory row by row as opposed to column by column. Left to right. One resentment at a time, one harm at a time, one romantic relationship at a time, one fear at a time. You may become tired or overwhelmed. You will find the strength to power through it. You may feel like not reading some of the items on your list. You will find the courage to be rigorously honest. You can do this. On the other side of this, you will be greatly rewarded for being thorough and honest.

When you are done reading your inventory, you will want to spend some time alone and reflect upon what you just went through. Open your mind and allow your thoughts to go where they may. Just witness them. Open your heart and allow yourself to feel any feelings that might arise. Allow them to run their course. Just witness them and let them go. Just allow yourself to be.

It takes a lot of courage to complete your Personal Inventory and read it to another human being. Every time we choose courage over fear, we strengthen the power of our courage and diminish the fear we have in our lives. Great fear requires great courage to overcome. You have taken a big step toward mastering yourself and mastering your fear.

FORGIVING OTHERS

I know I mentioned this before, but it is worth repeating here. "Having a resentment is like drinking poison and expecting someone else to get sick from it." By holding onto resentment or regret, we are creating negative consequences in our lives or hindering our growth in some fashion. We are hurting ourselves by holding onto resentments.

In completing your Personal Inventory, you have equipped yourself with a significant list of resentments and regrets. The first thing we need to do is make a separate list of all of these. Simply take them off your Personal Inventory and write them down in the Forgiveness worksheet provided at the end of this chapter. Put anyone on here you feel you need to forgive. The Forgiveness worksheet is very simple. Two columns, who you are forgiving, and what is being forgiven.

WHO NEEDS TO BE FORGIVEN?

Now you may be saying to yourself, "This person does not deserve my forgiveness," or, "How can I ever begin to forgive this person?" I understand. There were people in my inventory I didn't want to forgive either. You do not need to forgive someone if you do not want to. You can hold onto the entire experience for as long as you want to. Even if you have decided not to forgive them, put them on the list anyway. More is always being revealed.

ARE YOU WILLING TO FORGIVE THEM?

This does not mean you want to or know exactly how you will forgive this person. All this means is that you do not want to carry the pain any longer and will take the steps necessary to free yourself from it. All you need is a willingness to let go. You may not be willing to let go of some of these resentments yet.

And that's ok. Just know that when you are ready to let this go, there is a solution. We will focus on the ones you are willing to forgive. This will make a good beginning.

A key understanding you need to have is that these resentments are all rooted in your subconscious mind to one degree or another. Any lasting relief from these resentments will need to take place at the conscious and subconscious levels. Some you may be able to just let go of because you see the logic in doing so. It will still be prudent to take a couple of extra steps to ensure that it is completely removed from you.

The process I will describe to you can be approached in a couple of different ways depending on whether or not you believe in prayer. They both will allow you to forgive this person and fundamentally change your feelings toward this person. If you combine them, it makes the effect that much greater. The result you are looking for is freedom from the pain and negative influences of your resentment.

FORGIVENESS PROCESS: PRAY FOR THEM

The process is simple. This is the process I used to forgive those who had sexually assaulted me. Take out a piece of paper and write down all the things in your life that bring you happiness, joy, peace, love, and prosperity, and all the things you would like to have or do that would bring you more happiness, joy, peace, love, and prosperity. Imagine your best life.

Once you have written them down, take the time to fully associate with this ideal future you want. What do you see? What do you hear? What do you feel? Bring as much detail into it as you can. Make it as wonderful as you possibly can. Remember, your subconscious mind cannot distinguish between real or imagined thoughts, especially if the imagined thoughts have an intense kinesthetic quality to them.

When you feel like you have made this moment as wonderful as it can be, pray or hope that the person you have a resentment toward is receiving all these things. That's right. Pray something like this, "God, I wish that they have all the joy and happiness and love and prosperity that they can possibly have. That they might feel like I feel in my heart right now. If it is your will to do so, Lord, love them, bless them, may your grace fall upon them. Please take this wonderful feeling I have in my heart right now and give it to them, so that they might feel this feeling in this moment and be comforted by your perfect Light and Love."

The words will be different every time. The keys to this are to feel as wonderful as you can, maintain or increase that feeling throughout, all while holding the person to be forgiven in your heart and asking God to allow them to feel this feeling.

You don't even need to mean it, although if you do that helps. Just feeling that wonderful feeling and associating the person to be forgiven will create an association between the two. The two thoughts will fire and wire together.

Now, if you do not believe in prayer, simply visualize the other person as feeling as wonderful as you are right now. Visualize them as having all the things they need and desire to bring them as much peace and joy and love as they could possibly hope for.

Right now when you think about this person, you feel resentment toward them and all the pain, fears, unwanted thoughts, and emotions that go with it. This exercise will allow you to begin to associate this person with love, joy, and peace when you think about them. What you are doing with this exercise is creating a different conditioned response toward this person.

**You are changing the stimulus/response of thoughts of person = bad unwanted feelings
to
thoughts of person = good wanted feelings.**

Just like any conditioned response, it will take practice. Sometimes it just takes a couple of days. Sometimes a couple of weeks. This will depend on the strength of the resentment and your willingness to forgive them. Do this every day until you feel like either God has taken this resentment from you and allowed you to forgive this person, or you feel like you have effectively programmed yourself to think differently about this person and forgive them. You will know when this is done by feeling love and peace and joy automatically whenever you think about this person.

Remember, when you resent someone you are choosing to have negative feelings about something that happened in the past. We cannot control anything in the past because it doesn't exist any longer. It happened. It's over. The energy and power we choose to leave in the past by harboring resentment is just energy and power that we cannot use in the present to create a better tomorrow. The choice is yours to forgive them or not. There is no wrong answer. It takes what it takes. Things are what they are.

When it came time for me to forgive the two babysitters that sexually assaulted me as a child, it was difficult. I didn't even want to think about any of it. I tried to convince myself that it was over and nothing needed to be done about it. It was just something that happened. But the truth of the matter was that those assaults messed me up pretty bad. Looking at my Personal Inventory, I saw how they had influenced my self esteem and all the romantic relationships I had ever had. The damage was real, and part of me was really angry about it. It made me so sad to think that something like that caused me so much pain in my life. I had to let go. I had to forgive the situation and the two people involved. I applied this technique to both of them and the results have been pretty special. I also needed to forgive God for it. "How could you let this happen to me God?" My God and I are in pretty good standing now because I recognized the need to forgive. I harbored resentment. I was choosing to remain in pain. To not feel those feelings anymore is such a gift; I am eternally grateful.

I would like you to consider one more benefit before we move on to the next exercise. Every time you do this for the other person, you are experiencing these feelings yourself. You are experiencing the love. You are experiencing the joy. You are experiencing the peace. And you are experiencing the prosperity. In experiencing these, you are making these things true for you in that moment. You are blessing yourself at that moment. You are also telling your subconscious mind that you want and will have these things in your life. Our life becomes what we think about the most. We will touch on that a bit more in the chapters to come. Just know this exercise of forgiveness will benefit you and those around you in so many ways. And oh yeah, it feels really, really good.

MAKING AMENDS
We will now make a list of all the people, and groups of people, we may have harmed, and make amends to them. There are two types of amends. The "why" is very important. This is the path to self-forgiveness. It's great to be forgiven by them. To make things right with them and the universe and your Karma if you will. But we cannot control whether or not someone

forgives us. All we can control is whether or not we forgive ourselves. More on this a bit later.

DIRECT AMENDS

We apologize to them directly and make any restitution necessary.

INDIRECT AMENDS

If anyone will be hurt by us making direct amends, or if we cannot make direct amends for any reason, we can make indirect amends. Again, we will not be freeing ourselves from our own guilt at the expense of the person we are making amends to. Sometimes we need to get creative. If the person is no longer with us, or we cannot locate them, or the amends may hurt them, we can write a sincere letter of apology saying we are sorry and saying what we are sorry for. Say it out loud and then burn it. Or we can write the letter and we can do some charitable work for a day or a weekend and dedicate it to this person.

LIVING AMENDS

Although not on the worksheet, living amends are really a part of all amends. What does it mean if we say we are sorry and continue to do the same behaviors? It means nothing. That is an empty making of amends. I show that I'm sorry by correcting the behavior and not choosing to behave in that way any longer.

Most of my amends have been of this variety. I spoke and lived so many lies and exaggerated truths. I treated those around me in an unloving fashion. Although my loved ones in my life forgave me long before I was able to forgive myself, I continued to crucify myself for the things I had done. I loved them so much, but at times I didn't treat them like I did. Writing about it brings tears to my eyes. Not from regret or guilt or shame, but tears born from gratitude, gratitude that I have had the opportunities to make it right.

Life gives make-up tests. I have been working this program for long enough that I have been able to be a shining light in the lives of those I hurt. I have had ample opportunity to make what was done and said right. I have been given opportunities to be rigorously honest when to do so would be to my detriment. I have been given opportunities to be supportive and love my son, daughter, their mother, my parents, family and friends. I have also been given opportunities to love and be supportive to people that I did not know.

Any time you plan to make direct amends, run it by somebody else first to see if they think the amends may hurt the other person. Run it past a trusted adviser, good friend, therapist, clergyman, anyone that will not be afraid to give you an honest and objective opinion. It is of the utmost importance that we do not hurt anyone in any way by making amends.

The Amends worksheet is broken up into five columns: Who you need to make amends to, a detailed and precise account of exactly what it is you owe them amends for, direct amends or indirect amends, and amends completed. If indirect amends are to be made, write out what you intend to do.

This is an important step in freeing yourself from your past. You will no longer have to look over your shoulder. All the energy and power you had tied up in guilt, and regret, and resentments will be freed up, allowing you to focus your energy and power on positive changes in your life.

FORGIVING OURSELVES

We will now address all the regrets, shame, and remorse you have uncovered in your Personal Inventory. Forgiving ourselves involves four steps. I have provided a worksheet at the end of the chapter for this purpose.

We need to uncover what we need to forgive ourselves for. What do we regret doing or not doing?

We need to discover why we did what we did so we prevent it from happening again. What we are looking for here is what we were trying to gain.

This can include things like financial security, happiness, safety, sex, and power. This is sometimes called secondary gain or positive intention. Armed with this we can learn to attain these things in a more positive fashion. Simply ask yourself, "What did I gain by acting in this way?" This gain can be anything.

We need to discover any lessons we can learn from this. Ask yourself,

- "What can I take from this whole situation that is positive?"
- " What can I do differently next time to prevent this from happening again?"
- " What else can I do?"
- "Have I made amends, if appropriate?"
- "Is there anything else I need to do to make this right?"
- "Am I now willing to forgive myself?"

You have learned why you did what you did. You have learned any lesson you can take from this situation that will help you grow and help prevent this from happening again. You have done everything you could do to make this right. Now it's time to forgive yourself. Take a deep breath and let it go. If the feeling of regret comes up again, do not resist it. Witness it and ask yourself "What have I missed?" Sometimes these resurface for a reason. Pull this sheet out again and reassure yourself that you have done everything in your power to make this right. And then let it go. If it pops up again, as soon as you recognize it, fire your acceptance anchor and allow the peace and love in this state to dissolve any further regrets. Do this until it is gone forever.

I was sitting at my desk one morning doing a gratitude and love list. Out of nowhere, tears of joys poured down my face as I said out loud, "All the moments of my life have been forgiven." It is a precious gift to look back on your past and regret nothing, to be at complete peace with it. To look back and say you would not have changed a thing.

When we are mentally and emotionally caught up in the past, especially in a negative manner, we cannot enjoy the present moment, which is all that we ever truly have. The only time that is real is right now. Your life is happening right now, whether you are aware of it or not.

FORGIVENESS WORKSHEET

Who needs to be forgiven?	Are you willing to forgive them?

AMENDS WORKSHEET

Making Amends to	Specifics of amends	Direct	Indirect plan	Completed

PART 1: THE FREEDOM TO CHANGE

FORGIVING OURSELVES WORKSHEET

What I regret	Why I did it	Lessons to be learned	What else can I do?

CHAPTER 5

PART 2: THE POWER TO CHANGE YOUR PAST

In Part 1 of this chapter, you have done quite a bit of work on freeing up your power and focus from the past, so you can focus your power on the present and future. What you will be learning in Part 2 of this chapter is to use your perception of time to improve your life and influence your future in a positive way. You will be learning some powerful skills in this chapter that will allow you to:

- Control and alter your personal timeline.
- Heal your past from any lingering unwanted feelings.
- Look at the different phases of your life and reinforce all the good things that happened to you.

By learning these skills, you can gain control over your overall perception of your life. There is a learning curve to these skills as there has been with all the skills you have learned. Be patient with yourself. Celebrate every success. This is another one of those game-changing skills.

I will give you two quick examples of how many people perceive their personal timelines. There are two common types of timelines, and there are many variations of these two common types. One is sometimes called "in time." In this type, people imagine their past as behind them spatially, so they imagine their past events on an imaginary line behind them somewhere, they imagine their present in the area or space that their body occupies, and the future is out in front somewhere. The past can be in the front or back or at any angle intersecting with the body. They can be on a diagonal or go from low to high and or high to low.

The other common type is often referred to as "through time." This is where the imaginary timeline is out completely in front of them, beside them, or behind them. So, on a horizontal line you would have your past at one end, the future at the other, and your present somewhere in the middle.

Everyone's timeline is unique to them. Yours may be one of these, a combination of these, or something altogether different. A good way to think of it is, "if I could reach out and touch where I imagine this memory to be, where would that be?"

TIMELINE REIMPRINTING

I would like to start off with a personal story to illustrate how this next skill will benefit you. When I did my first Personal Inventory, like the one you did in the previous chapter, I wasn't exactly objective about how life had been up to that point. My perspective was clouded by fear, guilt, and shame. I was out of control when I was young. My teenage years were full of shameful acts and failures. The seventeen-year period around my first marriage was filled with memories of my insecurities, fears, and failures as a father and husband. My bout with alcoholism tainted that whole period of my life. This was the lens through which I viewed my past. When I looked at these periods of my life, the predominant feelings were negative.

By doing the work you have also done in this book, I have gained a more objective view of my past. I have put on a new pair of glasses if you will. I had so many wonderful moments and qualities as a boy and as a teenager. I found more good memories during my seventeen-year marriage than I could list here. It was an overwhelming number of blessings. I had a wonderful wife. She was an answer to one of my prayers. We were meant to be, just not meant to be forever. I was blessed with two wonderful healthy children. I loved my son and daughter, and they loved me. I did the best I could. I loved my parents, and they were always there for me, no matter what. I had wonderful in-laws and friends. I was successful in my career. We took nice vacations and lived in nice homes and drove nice cars. We had a lot of fun, and our lives were filled with a lot of love. And even when my drinking was at its worst, there was still love in my heart and people around me that never gave up on me and never stopped loving me. Yet, regardless of all the good in my life up to that point, it was all buried under that avalanche of fear, guilt, and shame.

When I look back on these periods of my life now, it is a great deal more balanced. It might be a bit more positive than it needs to be. I see I did a lot of good things in the past. And I did a lot of things I wish I hadn't. I see that I have for my whole life been exhibiting emotional and mental age-appropriate behavior. In so many instances I simply knew not what I did and did the best with what I knew and was at that moment.

I know that I am indeed a good person who, being human, made some mistakes and acted in an imperfect way. This has helped me in so many ways, especially with my self-esteem, self-confidence, and self-worth.

Have you ever heard anyone say something like "My teenage years were really painful," or, "My first marriage was absolutely horrible"? Or maybe something a little more subtle, like "My weekend sucked" or "I had a terrible day yesterday." As human beings, we key in on the negative. This is because the negatives are potential threats to our instincts. Whatever the reason may be, we take a period of time and label it as negative, failing to also represent the positives in that same period of time.

I still do this, although quite a bit less often as I used to. Last week I had a really great day filled with love and service and growth. That night I over-celebrated and ate some food I wasn't proud of eating. I fell short of the ideal. I took that feeling with me to bed that night. It wasn't horrible, but it wasn't objective. (If I had stuck to my evening program that night, which I will share with you later on in this book, I would have caught this.) I'm human. It's going to happen. If I hadn't looked back on that day and reframed it, I would have squandered the positives from that day that far outweighed the single negative.

EXERCISE: TIMELINE REIMPRINTING

Step 1: Remember your last bad day. Now imagine this bad day on your timeline. If you could touch it with your finger, where would it be? Now notice the submodalities about it, (brightness, size, color, motion, etc.). Notice if anything jumps out at you. Making out memories on a timeline can be difficult, let alone recognizing the VAK and submodalities. You will get better at this with practice. All you need for any of this is a general sense of how you perceive your timeline spatially. Just remember that.

Now take out a blank piece of paper and draw a line across it to represent your timeline for that day. Take yourself through the day and write in all the positives of that day. Sometimes it can be difficult when looking at a single day. Some days carry with them a high degree of difficulty. I get it. When I am doing this on a difficult day, I like to start with a few not-so-obvious positives like, I woke up that morning, or I wasn't homeless that day, or I didn't starve that day. This usually opens me up enough to remember the times I laughed or smiled that day. I remember if I was kind to anyone that day. I remember if I was kind to myself that day. I remember if I held anyone in my heart and loved them that day. Did I exhibit any positive traits? Did I eat healthily? Did I get in some good exercise? If I worked that day, did I get paid for it? These are just some ideas. Look at your day and if you can remember anything positive that happened, plot it at the appropriate time on your timeline for the day.

Now remember the best day you can remember, and imagine it on your timeline like you did the "bad" day. Notice the VAK. Notice if there were any differences. Write down the VAK from your good day (brightness, size, color, motion, etc.). Or it could just be an emotional quality.

Now, look at the sheet you have in front of you that you charted your bad day on. See it within the framework of your good day's VAK. For example, if you saw your good day as larger or brighter or sharper or louder than your bad day, imagine this timeline in front of you as being larger or brighter or sharper or louder than it was. Allow that all to settle in. Allow yourself to feel this bad day as a good day. When I looked at my bad day, I made it larger and then associated with it, reliving it like I did the good days. It became life-sized, followed by good, positive feelings.

Now take that day and place it back on your timeline where the bad day was. See the differences. Feel the difference. In a couple of hours, remember that day again. You don't have to imagine it on your timeline if you don't want to. Just see if that changed the way you feel about that day.

Step 2: Now that you are familiar with this process, it's time to try it on a larger "bad" time in your life; a month, or maybe a year. Any larger period of life with a negative feel to it. Imagine it on your timeline. Write down the VAK that is present.

Draw a timeline on a piece of paper that represents this period in your life. If it helps, imagine you are taking that whole period off of your timeline and laying it over the piece of paper. Now write in all the positive things you can remember about that period. They don't have to have anything to do with the reason you labeled it bad. For instance, if the period is bad because of a horrible job, you can put in good things about the job, but you can also put in there anything else positive that happened in any other area of your life during that period. When you look back at that period of your life, you may have omitted them because of the negative experience of the job. They could be anything. Relationships. Accomplishments. Time with friends and family. Maybe you were happy and content with your health. Maybe there was a vacation that you thoroughly enjoyed. If you have positive feelings about those memories, allow yourself to feel them now. Write in as many as you want. Feel good about that period of your life.

In a couple of hours, think back to that period. Not just the content; for example, a bad relationship, but the whole period of time. See if it feels any better.

It can be difficult to do. I get it. When I used this technique on my teenage years it was very difficult to find anything positive about it. I fought with addiction when I was a teenager. I fought. I stole. I dropped out of the eighth grade. And that's when it got really bad. Crystal methamphetamine was a part of the following five years of my life, with all the shameful things that can bring. There were so many moments of feeling utter worthlessness and shame.

But when I applied this technique, I was able to see that period differently. My family loved me. I had good friends that I loved. For the most part, I was healthy physically, as I was addicted to working out as well. I met the woman who would eventually bless me with two wonderful children. There were a couple of prayers that were answered in that time that I never recognized before doing this exercise. I knew not what I did. I was just a kid. I can now use that period of my life as a source of great strength and faith. God never gave me anything I couldn't handle. What didn't kill me made me stronger. There is now a great understanding of the fact that it takes what it takes. Everything that was must have been. There could not have been any other way.

Now remember one of the best periods of your life you can remember. Choose a similar length of time. For example, if it was a bad winter, choose a good season or three-month period. If a period was bad because of a bad relationship, your good time period doesn't need to include a good relationship, although that would make it doubly powerful if it did. Whatever it is, imagine it on your timeline. Notice how you see it, hear it, and feel it. If you can, imagine taking that period and, like you did the bad time period, overlaying the timeline in front of you with it. Adjust the bad timeline in front of you to match the characteristics of the good period of time. See the good moments in it. Hear the good moments in it. Feel the good moments in it. Then pick it up and insert it back into your timeline.

Step 3: You can do this for whole decades. Whole childhoods. Any period of your life. A key thing to remember is when you imagine that period, you are not just keyed in on one aspect of it like a specific job or relationship or health issue. You are treating the entire period. You are finding the good that has always been there, that you haven't been giving yourself credit for, because of the negative aspect of that period. You may find that the way you perceive your decades on a timeline is far different than how you perceive a year, or a month. For instance, I see a decade as a horizontal string three feet in front of my body, with the clocklike years hanging on that, and my monthly and weekly timelines drop down into actual calendars. Experience your timeline in whatever framework it presents itself. See it. Hear it. Feel it. Experience it.

Choose at least one larger period of time and apply the same process to it as you did with the smaller period and the bad day. If it's a decade, make sure to break it down year by year, month by month if you can. Challenge yourself to find at least ten good things about each year.

After you have done this with a few periods of time, notice any patterns with the positive periods in your life. Ask yourself:

- If they have a common color to them, what would that color be?
- If they have a common size or brightness, what would that be?

- If they have a common sound or volume, what would that be?
- If they have a common vibration or feeling about them, what would that be?

Notice any common traits. What you are looking for is anything you can add to large periods of your timeline. For instance, if while imagining your timeline you notice that most positive periods have a slight white light about them, write that down. You can use that to change the "color" or "brightness" of larger periods, past or future. If you have found nothing, try asking your subconscious this question: "I am speaking now to my subconscious. (Pause.) If the positive moments of my life did have a common characteristic, what would that be?" And wait for the answer.

When you have gotten good at this, you can simply look back on a period of your life that isn't as good as you want it to be and continue to remember good things about that period. You can also make broad adjustments to periods. This does not replace the actual itemizing of the good memories and plotting them on your timeline. The broad adjustments will just work to enhance it.

The past is over. It doesn't exist anymore, yet it will continue to influence you, good or bad, for the rest of your life. All the moments of your past can bind you and hold you back and keep you down, or they can propel you forward and inspire you and set you free to become the person you want to become and live the life you have always wanted to live. Your past doesn't have to be something that happened to you. It can be something that has happened for you. The choice is yours.

TIMELINE CLEANSING

You have done a lot of work on learning the lessons your past held for you and freeing your energy and power from it. Timeline Cleansing is another tool you can put in your toolbox that will allow you to continue to grow and improve the quality of your life; past, present, and future.

Some of the common emotions that people cleanse their timelines of are anger, sadness, fear, anxiety, hurt, guilt, low self-esteem, etc. You can use this technique on any troublesome emotion. One fear that I used this technique on was my fear of confrontation. This stemmed from an incident when I was a child. When I was in the third grade, Mr. Blumer's class at Sherwood Forest Elementary School in Bellevue, Washington, I was beat up by Mitch, the largest third grader ever. I remember it as if it was yesterday. All of my human interactions since applying this technique to that event have changed for the better because I applied this technique to that moment. It's amazing how an unrealistic fear of getting punched in the face had influenced my life in situations where there was no possibility that I would've been punched in the face.

There are a lot of things happening behind the scenes in this exercise. Everyone's experience will be different. You may find some spiritual feelings of healing and forgiveness. You may feel like you are reintegrating parts of you that have been frozen in time, standing guard protecting you from the perceived danger in that moment. Whatever you experience will be exactly what you need to experience.

Anytime you introduce an intense kinesthetic component and more evolved consciousness to these memories, you change them. You cannot change the facts about these situations. You can change how you feel about them. Every time you do this, you change it some more. Remember, neurons that fire together, wire together.

In this exercise, I will guide you back to your first memory of the situation that caused the unwanted emotion. (Like me being punched in the face in the third grade.) You need to realize that, as you have experienced similar events since this moment, you may have triggered this emotional response. It doesn't even need to be exactly like this situation. It could just be similar. What you are looking for is the template you have been using to respond to situations like this. You're looking for ground zero. When you change this template, you change the way you respond to similar situations moving forward.

EXERCISE: TIMELINE CLEANSING

Please familiarize yourself with this complete process before beginning. It would be preferable if you did this with a partner. They can walk you through this, and you can return the favor. Or record the steps and play them back to yourself. Just make sure you give yourself enough time between steps.

Step 1: The first thing you want to do is settle on how you want to experience your timeline for this exercise. The nice thing about timelines is that they are flexible. Just have a good, clear perception for this.

Step 2: Choose the unwanted emotion you will work on. Let's say that it's anger. Close your eyes and remember the most recent time you felt this feeling and imagine it on your timeline. Think about this moment until you feel a little taste of the anger. Now travel back through time, stopping at all the memories that pop up in which you felt this feeling. No need to struggle. Just relax and let your subconscious take you on a ride. Do this until you come to your first memory of ever feeling this way. Do your best not to consciously control this. Just allow it to happen. This can take some time.

Step 3: When you have come to your first memory of this emotion, stand just before it in time, facing back toward your present, and observe it for a moment. See your younger self at that moment. Now become very aware of all the wisdom and insight you have gained since you experienced that moment.

Now ask your subconscious:

- Are there any lessons to be learned here?
- Are there any opportunities for growth in this moment?
- What resources is this earlier version of us lacking?
- What current understanding and wisdom do we have that would help us in this moment?
- Have we learned what we needed to learn?
- Is it ok now that we can move on from this moment and not feel like this anymore?

You are looking for an affirmative feeling or verbal response here.

Step 4: Now it's time for the younger "you" trapped in this moment to "grow up." Making sure you are associated in this younger version of yourself, bring into your experience all the lessons you have learned about this emotion in your entire life, all the growth you have had since this moment, all the wisdom and positive feelings that are present.

Next, pick yourself up and allow yourself to settle down into that earlier moment you felt this emotion for the first time, bringing all the growth and knowledge and positive emotion into that moment. See the things you saw in that moment that triggered the emotion, hear the things you heard in that moment that triggered the emotion, and bring into it this new feeling and wisdom and everything that comes with it. Stay here if it feels right to do so. Again, your subconscious is running the show. Be very aware of any promptings or inspiration.

When you are ready, while still fully associated, invite this earlier version of yourself to come experience all the moments of your life with you. You are now the nurturing parent. Invite it to grow up with you. Now, "grow up" through time, bringing your earlier self and this new feeling and wisdom with you. When other occurrences of this emotion present themselves on your timeline, stop and bring this new feeling and wisdom into each moment. Each time, ask your subconscious if you have anything else to learn from this moment. Take your time with this. Be open-minded and willing to allow yourself to feel any emotions that arise. If you do not allow yourself to feel these emotions, they will continue to influence your life. Be willing to allow yourself to pop in and out of your timeline and the memories as needed. This is very much an act of being and allowing, not doing. Sometimes when I do this, it is a straight shot forward through time from past to present, like the moments are flowing through the center of my chest. Sometimes I pop in and out, go back, jump out to the side, and all manner of different deviations. Just hold the newfound wisdom and feeling in your heart and mind and allow whatever happens to happen. Do this until you are back in the present moment.

Step 5: Test it. Think back on some of those moments that caused the feeling. Notice how you feel. Imagine a similar situation happening in the future. Notice how you feel at that moment. Be prepared to write down any insights or inspiration. Sometimes wisdom will come that has nothing to do with the emotion that you just "grew up."

If there is still some lingering emotion, there may be an earlier instance of this emotion, or variations of this emotion stemming from a different incident. If so, then run through these steps again. After I did this a few times, this process began to happen automatically. I would find the cause of an unwanted belief, thought, emotion, or behavior and the healing would automatically make its way back to the present. On its way, like falling dominoes, it would change the meaning of all the related moments in its path. It's like my subconscious said, "I see what you're doing. Sit back and relax. I got this."

I know a lot of this might seem a little foreign and different. And that's good. Different is good. We're here because we want to grow. If we do the same thing over and over again all we will ever get is the same results. Here are some good tips for you.

Suspend any judgment.

Go into it intending to grow with the positive expectancy you will find relief from this unwanted emotion.

When you are in these moments, bring as much detail and intensity of positive emotion as you can. Bring as much growth and wisdom and understanding as you possibly can into that moment. What you are doing is reprogramming the memory with a different kinesthetic quality. The facts about the moment remain the same; you just feel differently about it now, thus allowing you to respond differently to memories of this situation and similar situations moving forward.

Use this skill with as many emotions as you like. You may find that when you "grow up" a younger version of yourself through your timeline, there are positive effects on other emotions as well. These situations we are bringing this new wisdom and understanding and growth into often carry within them multiple unwanted emotions.

PART 2: THE POWER TO CHANGE YOUR PAST

CHAPTER 5 KEY TAKEAWAYS

- By reading your Personal Inventory out loud to another human being you create the pressure and heat required to begin freeing yourself from your past.
- By forgiving yourself and others and making amends, you free your power and focus from these mental, emotional, and spiritual entanglements.
- We all perceive time in our own unique way.
- We can change the way we perceive our timeline if it benefits us.
- We can go back into our past and turn "bad" periods into "good" periods.
- We can bring our current level of consciousness, understanding, growth, and wisdom into the moments of our past, helping our younger self to grow up.

CHAPTER 6

THE POWER TO CHANGE YOUR BEHAVIORS

"Real change, enduring change,
happens one step at a time."

~RUTH BADER GINSBERG

In the previous five chapters, you have increased your awareness of how your character traits, beliefs, thoughts, fears, emotions, and behaviors have affected your life. To simplify things for this chapter, we will call all these "behaviors." You understand that your life results directly from all these things and that if you continue to think and act as you have, you will continue to get the same results you have been getting. If you want to change, then you must focus on the cause. That is what you will do in this chapter. In this chapter, you will increase your understanding and awareness of your more bothersome unwanted behaviors and deliberately choose what behaviors you would like to strengthen or create for yourself.

PART 1: UNWANTED BEHAVIORS

In the previous chapters, you have worked diligently to uncover your unwanted behaviors. You have looked at these from many angles: What you did, why you did it, what situations they occurred in, your fears connected to them, how they have affected others, and what you would do differently.

To begin this exercise, take out a blank piece of paper and write down all the unwanted behaviors and all your fears from your Personal Inventory. Don't worry about categorizing them or prioritizing them, as you will be doing that later on in the exercise. If you think of any that were not on your inventory, you can write them down now. Your fears inventory is cut and dry, but the rest can be harder to identify. It's difficult to find things when you don't know what you are looking for, so below, I have listed some examples for you to choose from. This is not a complete list by any stretch of the imagination, but it should point you in the right direction and give you some ideas of things you have the power to change. I know to some degree or another, at one time or another, consciously or unconsciously, I exhibited a good many of these behaviors in my life.

- Selfishness
- Impatience
- Dishonesty
- Laziness
- False pride
- Undisciplined
- Greed
- Insecurity
- Gluttony
- Low self-confidence

- Lust
- Rudeness
- Unfriendliness
- Arrogance
- Procrastination
- Self-loathing
- Self-hatred
- Low self-esteem
- Hate
- Lack of self-control
- Resentment
- Manipulativeness
- Regret
- Smoking
- Self-pity
- Overeating
- Envy
- Drugs/alcohol
- Disrespect
- Infidelity
- Intolerance
- Gossip

At the end of this chapter, there is a Desired Behaviors Worksheet. Take your top five unwanted behaviors and list them in order in column one. Hang on to any extras you may have. Once you learn the process, you can apply it to them and any others that might pop up.

PART 2: SECONDARY GAIN OR POSITIVE INTENT

The second column on the Desired Behaviors worksheet is secondary gain or positive intent. These presuppose that any bad behavior has, or is meant to have, some type of positive outcome. These are the desired outcomes we are hoping to create by using our unwanted behaviors. The behaviors are just a means to an end.

EXAMPLES OF SECONDARY GAIN

Smoking: The secondary gain might be that one may smoke to relax, or increase focus, or fit in, or to ease their boredom.

Alcohol/Drug Abuse: The secondary gain might be to numb physical or emotional pain, or to fit in, or to feel confident or secure, or to have a better time.

Fears: The secondary gain of most fears is to keep us safe and secure. They may protect us from feeling the pain of rejection, or protect us from losing a job, etc.

A child's tantrum: The secondary gain might be to gain attention, or communicate a painful emotion, or to feel secure.

Gossip: The secondary gain might be to feel important, better about oneself, to fit in or give themselves a better sense of security within a social group.

Overeating: The secondary gain might be emotional comfort, or to ease boredom, or could be a cry for help.

Exaggerating: The secondary gain might be to fit in, or be loved, or to be thought of as important, or to increase one's standing in the eyes of others.

Sex: If sex is a problem, then the secondary gain might be that one is using sex to feel secure, or to control someone, or to feel adequate, or prop up one's self-esteem, etc.

Dishonesty: The secondary gain from this might be to feel safe and secure in one's employment, to feel important, or feel cool and accepted by their peers.

I have experienced all of these to one degree or another in my life. As everyone experiences life differently, the secondary gain can be anything. I hope these examples have shown you what you are looking for.

A key presupposition (something assumed to be true) of NLP is that people always make the best choice they are aware they have at any given time. In discovering what the secondary gains of your unwanted behaviors are, you can work on finding healthier, more productive methods of achieving the same desired outcome. You can give yourself more choices, which is always an advantage. When we feel stuck or trapped in a situation, it's often because we either don't like the choices we have or are simply unaware that we have choices.

You may also find that the secondary gain involved is no longer of any importance to you. This awareness alone can take away a lot of the sticking power of some of these unwanted behaviors. In column two of your Desired Behaviors worksheet, you can write in all the secondary gains you come up with. Sometimes the secondary gain is not readily apparent. Give it time. It will surely come.

PART 3: SECONDARY GAIN REFRAMING

Now that you have found the secondary gain or positive intention of your unwanted behaviors, you can find better ways of achieving the desired outcome. The exercise below will help you do just that.

Step 1: Identify the unwanted behaviors.

Step 2: Identify the secondary gain. Recognize the value in this gain and thank yourself for wanting that for yourself. This may sound strange, but actually say the words out loud, "Thank you for wanting (secondary gain) for us. That is important to me. I appreciate it very much."

By being grateful and positive, you are trying to bypass any fear-based resistance to change. Remember, we will usually choose a painful known quantity over the fear of the unknown or change. By speaking to yourself, you include the part of you creating or holding onto these unwanted behaviors. You are allowing it to feel important, needed, and in control. What you are doing here is called a type of "parts" work. This "part" of you is almost always in your subconscious mind.

A few examples of what that might look like:
When I smoked, my secondary gains were:

- To feel relaxed or as a reason to take a break at work. To fit in with the group. To not be bored. To stay sharp mentally.

When I drank, my secondary gains were:

- To avoid feeling insecure. To feel safe through escape. To fit in with others. To not be bored. And euphoria.

When exaggerating the truth, my secondary gains were:

- To be liked and accepted. To feel secure in my job. Financial security. To not get in trouble. To feel good about myself.

Step 3: Ask yourself out loud, "If there were better ways to accomplish/attain/feel (secondary gain), would you be interested in discovering them?" What you are looking for here is an actual voice in your head saying yes or an affirmative feeling in your body. If it's an absolute no (you will feel resistance toward the idea), return to Step 2 and see if you have the secondary gain right. Then repeat Step 3.

Step 4: Come up with as many alternative choices as you can. It doesn't matter if it's a viable option or not. Just allow yourself to brainstorm and come up with as many options as you can.

Step 5: Choose your three favorite alternative behaviors and imagine yourself using these in a situation you normally would have responded to with your unwanted behaviors. Take the time to immerse yourself in it. See what you see. Hear what you hear. Feel what you feel as you are achieving the secondary gain with this new choice. Your subconscious mind does not know the difference between real or imagined. All it will see is that you succeeded with this new choice and will be more willing to do it again.

Step 6: Ask yourself, "Would I have any objection to using these new methods moving forward to accomplish (secondary gain)?" And "Do I feel like these choices will allow me to feel (secondary gain) moving forward?" Again, be aware of any resistance to these choices.

You have now given your conscious and subconscious mind alternative choices it can now use instead of the unwanted behavior. Insert the alternative choices you came up with in column three of the Desired Behaviors worksheet.

Now take a moment and look at your column two and three. What insight can you gain? Are your secondary gains revealing anything to you? For example, if my unwanted behavior were bragging, and my secondary gain was to feel emotionally secure by receiving validation from others, I might ask myself why I am making my emotional security dependent on the opinions and approval of others. As we know, we cannot control other people, so to rely upon them for our own well-being is a recipe for disappointment.

Looking at your column two and three, ask yourself where you are seeking outside validation and where you are making your well-being contingent upon things you cannot control. Keep any insights or understanding this affords you in mind as you begin Part 4.

PART 4: WANTED BEHAVIORS

You now have increased your understanding of what your unwanted behaviors are as well as gained an understanding of some reasons why you were choosing those behaviors. Now it's time to consider the behaviors you would like to replace the old ones with.

Now consider each of the unwanted behaviors you have and ask yourself, "In what contexts am I typically using these? What is the trigger that elicits the unwanted behavioral response?" Get clear on this and write it down on a separate piece of paper. This is slightly redundant to the previous exercise, but we want to become aware of our triggers. As our awareness of our triggers increases and improves, our ability to insert a pause in between the trigger and our old unwanted response will increase. We can then more readily insert a wanted behavior.

Examples of finding the trigger for an unwanted behavior would be: If my unwanted behavior were impatience, my trigger could be sitting in traffic, or waiting in line at the store, or my kids not understanding what I am trying to tell them. Each different trigger is considered a context.

What would be your desired behaviors, or desired response to each of these triggering events? Remember that the desired behavior does not need to be the opposite of the unwanted behavior, or have any relation to the unwanted behavior, for that matter. This exercise is meant to teach you that if you do not like the way you are reacting to a certain situation, you can change it. Write your wanted behaviors in column four of the Desired Behaviors worksheet.

Hopefully by completing these worksheets you've been given a greater understanding of how behaviors have been controlling and shaping your life thus far. Moving forward, when presented with a trigger, you will be able to pause and choose how you would like to proceed, as opposed to just reacting to the trigger with the same old unwanted behavior.

CHAPTER 6 KEY TAKEAWAYS

- We all have unwanted behaviors.

- All our unwanted behaviors have a secondary gain or positive intent. This is why we choose to do the things that we do. It is our true motive.

- You can find other ways of accomplishing the same positive intent that are wanted and positive and in alignment with who you want to be and the life you want to live.

- We do not have to react to triggers any longer. We can intentionally and consciously respond to those triggers however we want to.

DESIRED BEHAVIOR WORKSHEET

Unwanted Behaviors	Secondary Gain or Positive Intent	Alternative methods of achieving secondary gain	Wanted Behaviors

CHAPTER 7

YOUR IDEAL SELF

"Find a beautiful piece of art. If you fall in love with Van Gogh or Matisse or John Oliver Killens, or if you fall in love with the music of Coltrane, the music of Aretha Franklin, or the music of Chopin, find some beautiful art and admire it, and realize that it was created by human beings just like you, no more human, no less."

~ MAYA ANGELOU

In the previous six chapters, you have learned quite a bit about yourself. You have done a lot of work and have begun to make positive changes in yourself and your life. The transformational techniques and understandings you have learned thus far, these tools you will strengthen and be able to use for the rest of your life, have given you the ability to consciously, deliberately, and intentionally become the person you want to become.

We have focused a lot on uncovering our unwanted character traits, discovering the lessons and wisdom within them, clearing up any lingering negative effects of these traits, and we have developed the skills necessary to create a new set of character traits moving forward. We have focused a lot on what wasn't working for us, which was necessary to create profound and lasting change in our lives. The main purpose of the previous six chapters was to allow you to stop looking back and start looking forward.

In this chapter, you will create, in great detail and with great intensity, the ideal self you will aspire to become. You will powerfully shift your focus to what you like about yourself and who you have always wanted to be. In this chapter, you will be the architect of your Ideal Self.

CREATING YOUR IDEAL SELF

A presupposition of NLP is "Anyone can do anything." It is an assumption that if it is possible, and if someone has already done it, then it can be modeled and recreated. To accomplish the same thing, you would need to study the person who has done it and discover what qualities, mindsets, techniques, knowledge, and skills the person used to accomplish what you would like to accomplish. Then you work diligently at duplicating the approach until you succeed. NLP calls this "modeling." You will use modeling in this chapter to create a set of ideal character traits you want to embody. These character traits are the foundation of your ideal self.

IDENTIFY YOUR STRENGTHS

A character trait is a characteristic pattern of thoughts, feelings, and behaviors. Traits are consistent and stable and operate across a broad range of situations. They are a fundamental part of who we are and how we respond to life. No matter who we are, or what our lives look like, we all have unwanted traits we would like to overcome. No one is perfect. On the flip side of that coin, we also all have innate strengths and talents. Some of these we are aware of, and some we are not. Some have been developed and honed and others have not. In this section, we will be looking at the traits you have that you would like to develop and strengthen and include in the model of your ideal self.

I have provided an Ideal Traits worksheet. The first column is set aside for the current character traits you are strong in. Take out a blank piece of paper and write in big letters at the top of the page, "What traits do I like most about myself?"

I would like you to relax, take a few deep breaths, and allow yourself to think of times in your life you were really happy with yourself. Times you felt good about yourself. Immerse yourself in everything that you like about yourself. Allow yourself to write down anything that comes to mind. Do not censor this in any way. Just allow yourself to write whatever comes to mind. Write in all the positive character traits you see most often in yourself.

This is not the time to be "humble" but a time for "humility." You are not more than or less than anyone else. You are no more or less than you believe you should be; just how you are and how you have been. Not a glass of water half empty or half full. Just a glass with some water in it. If you are terrific at something, write that down. If you have a kind heart, write that down. Whatever you excel at or have excelled at, write that down. Allow yourself to give credit where credit is due. Allow yourself to celebrate you. I happen to think you are beyond special and wonderful.

IDEAL TRAITS MODELING WORKSHEET

Current positive traits and talents	Desired traits and talents	Who I admire most	Traits and talents I want to model

Here is a list of common character traits to give you an idea of what you are looking for. This list will also help to create your wanted traits, so if you see anything that you do not have that you would like to develop, underline it or highlight it. We will come back to that later.

If what you want is not below, write it down anyways. Like when I ran this list past my daughter she said, "Dad. Conquering the world isn't down there," which I loved, and there is nothing wrong with that. That is the good stuff. The quirky, funny things that make us who we are. Be who you choose to be because you have the sincere desire to be so. Somebody famous said, "To thine own self be true."

While reading this list aloud, you might pause with each word, allow yourself the time to contemplate the meaning of each word, and allow yourself to remember times when you might have exhibited these traits in your life.

- Honest
- Quick learner
- Courageous
- Athletic
- Humble
- Intelligent
- Generous
- Passionate
- Calm
- Fair
- Patient
- Hardworking
- Tolerant
- Loyal
- Considerate
- Funny
- Forgiving
- Motivated
- Loving
- Disciplined
- Empathetic
- Open-minded
- Modest
- Reliable

- Trustworthy
- Kind
- Faithful
- Creative
- Respectful
- Strong
- Friendly
- Confident
- Good listener
- Determined
- Resilient
- Persistent
- Selfless
- Balanced

List is the traits you are strong in and the traits you have that you would like to develop. Now you will rank the traits on your piece of paper in order of importance and strength. Choose the one that is the most important and write a "1" next to it. Then, the one next in importance, write a "2" next to it, etc. When you have completed this, enter them, in that order, in column one of your Ideal Traits Modeling worksheet.

IDENTIFY YOUR DESIRED TRAITS

Column two in your Ideal Traits worksheet is for the traits you would like to create and develop within yourself. Taking out your sheet again, write all your desired traits in column two. Refer now to your Personal Inventory worksheets if you need to, particularly the ideal columns, and see if there are any traits in these worksheets you would like to add to column two. When the first two steps are done, ask yourself, "What am I missing from this sheet? What is important to me that is not represented here?" Allow yourself the time to wait for the answers.

When you feel like you have written down everything you need to write down, you will rank these in order of importance and strength like you did in column one. Choose the one that is the most important and write a "1" next to it. Then, the one next in importance, write a "2" next to it, etc. When you have this down, enter them, in that order, in column two of your Ideal Traits Modeling worksheet.

IDENTIFY THE PEOPLE YOU WOULD LIKE TO MODEL
What we are looking for here is the people you admire the most. People who "have something" that you want. These people could be celebrities, leaders in your current field of work or a field you would like to get into, spiritual leaders, thought leaders, politicians, or historical figures. It can be anyone you hold in high esteem, who you would like as a role model; someone you would like to emulate. I chose people like Martin Luther King Jr., Anthony Robbins, Napoleon Hill, James Allen, Oprah Winfrey, Jesus Christ, Barack Obama, and Buddha to name a few.

Now take out another piece of paper and draw a line down the center as you did before. At the top of the left side, write, "Who I admire," and at the top of the right side, write, "What I admire about them."

Starting with the left column, allow yourself to relax and take a few deep breaths. Now open your mind and brainstorm the people you currently admire and people you have admired in the past. Ask yourself, "Who are the people that I have admired most in my life?" Remember that some of these people may exhibit multiple traits you would like to strengthen or develop.

When you are done with this, you will rank these in order of importance and strength. When you rank these, consider role models with multiple traits you would like to develop. Choose the one that is the most important and write a "1" next to it. Then, the one next in importance, write a "2" next to it, etc. When you have this down, enter them in that order column three of your Ideal Traits Modeling worksheet.

Now turn your attention to the right column of the brainstorm page, "What I admire about them." This exercise will not be a classic brainstorm. The things you put on this side of the page will be much more precise and deliberate.

Start by relaxing, taking a few deep breaths, and bringing into your mind your #1 ranked individual. From the neutral observer perspective, imagine them in as much detail as you can. When you can see them clearly, ask yourself, "What character traits does this person have that I would like to develop in myself?" Write your answers to this question in column four of your Ideal Traits Modeling worksheet next to the #1 person. Repeat this process with all the people you have listed.

MODELING CURRENT AND DESIRED TRAITS

I have provided a Trait Anchoring worksheet for you. Consider your Ideal Traits Modeling worksheet and choose up to five character traits, either ones you already have that you would like to strengthen or ones you want to develop. Anything more than that can be overwhelming. When you feel good about the first five, you can use the following process on the rest of them. In order of importance, write down your five desired traits in column one.

Next, look at the people you admire. Which ones exhibit the trait you are looking to work on? In column two, write all the people you want to model for each trait.

YOUR IDEAL SELF

TRAIT ANCHORING WORKSHEET

Ideal Character Traits	People who exemplify this trait	Detail of their model	Future Pace Situations

EXERCISE: ANCHOR STACKING

Now comes the fun part. This is powerful. We will use a technique called Anchor Stacking. You will be creating an anchor as you did before with the acceptance anchor, but we will be adding multiple experiences to increase the intensity of it. Before you begin, choose a place to create your physical anchor. For this exercise, I touched my left thumb to the second knuckle of my left pinky finger. Regardless of what you choose, make sure you are keeping track of these anchors. I use a three-by-five card to index them and have a separate notebook with the modalities and submodalities listed for each anchor.

I was talented at speaking in front of an audience but was still very afraid to do so. I applied this exercise to that. Now, when I activate my anchor, I am mentally onstage in a medium-sized auditorium. My body breaks out in goosebumps as the energy flows through it. My posture straightens and my mind softens. My breathing slows, and the anxiety and fear turn into excitement and gratitude and humility. So very grateful for the opportunity to stand in front of those beautiful people and share my experience, strength, and hope with them. There is a deep breath, and then, on the exhale, there is peace. I now use this anchor in many circumstances, sometimes for no reason at all but to feel really good. I am humbled by it. It is such a gift to be able to feel this way anytime and anywhere. Please give yourself that gift now.

Starting with a current trait you want to strengthen (if not a current trait, then move on to the next step in this process). Remember a time when you strongly embodied this trait. Relive this moment in as much detail as possible. Write down the details in column 3. The details you are looking for are:

- **Visual-** Location of image, size, is it framed like a TV or panoramic, black and white or color, moving or still, associated (seeing through your eyes) or dissociated (seeing as if a neutral observer)
- **Auditory-** Volume, Speed, Location, Tonality
- **Kinesthetic-** Location of feeling, shape, movement, pressure, color

Also, bring into your awareness these considerations.

- Your posture.
- What is your breathing like?
- How are you holding your head?
- What about your facial gestures?
- What are you doing with your arms and your hands?
- Are you moving?
- Anything else of note you are aware of?

Once you have written these down in column three, turn your attention to this moment and feel what you feel and listen for anything you might be saying to yourself. Take some time to feel this character trait as much as possible. What would happen if this feeling doubled? Tripled? Do whatever you can to amplify the trait, and when you are at its peak, set and hold your anchor, releasing it when you feel it decreasing. Now break your state.

If you have any other memories of times when you embodied this trait, apply the process again to that memory. You will use the same anchor. This is "stacking anchors."

Now take a person you want to model. The process for

this will be similar to what you just did and you will use the same anchor. Imagine a time when this person was exhibiting this wanted trait. Imagine this in as much detail as possible. Write down the details in column three. Details you are looking for are the same as before:

- **Visual-** Location of image, size, is it framed like a TV or panoramic, black and white or color, moving or still, associated (seeing through your eyes) or dissociated (seeing as if a neutral observer)
- **Auditory-** Volume, Speed, Location, Tonality
- **Kinesthetic-** Location of feeling, shape, movement, pressure, color

Also bring into your awareness these considerations.

- Their posture.
- What is their breathing like?
- How are they holding their head?
- What about their facial gestures?
- What are they doing with their arms and hands?
- Are they moving?
- Anything else of note you are aware of?

Write these details down in column three. Now fully turn your attention to this moment, associating into this person and imagining how they are experiencing this trait. Imagine you are them. Take some time to settle in. See what they see. Are they saying anything to themselves? Are they saying anything out loud? Bring all the details you wrote in column three into your awareness. Match their posture. Match their breathing; duplicate their physiology as much as you can. Imagine as much as you can how this person feels while exhibiting this trait. What are they thinking? Consider everything you know about this person. Be this person. Do whatever you can to amplify the trait. Can you double it? Triple it? When it is at its peak, set and hold the same anchor, releasing it when you feel it decreasing. Now break your state.

Repeat this process with all the people you have listed for this trait.

Now test your anchor. Remember Hebb's Law, "Cells that fire together, wire together." The more you practice this anchor, the stronger the new set of connections become. The stronger the new set of connections becomes, the more automatic this new trait will become.

Keep an eye out as well for strong examples of people exemplifying any of these traits. If so, write down everything you can in as much detail as you can. If you cannot write it down, then take a mental snapshot. Then apply this exercise again and stack it on the appropriate anchor.

FUTURE PACE YOUR ANCHORS

To be courageous, you need to act courageously. If you want more patience, then you need to be more patient. To be calmer, you need to practice being calm. If you want more energy, then you need to practice being energetic. Remember, your subconscious mind cannot distinguish between real or imagined experiences, especially if they are intense. You don't need to wait months or years to develop these new traits. Michael Jordan didn't practice making the game-winning shot during the actual game. He shot thousands of practice shots per week so that during the real game when it really counted, he was as prepared as he possibly could be. You don't have to react to life if you don't want to. You can strengthen these traits by practicing them so when life happens, as it surely will, you can respond to it how you want to, rather than reacting to it—repetition, repetition, repetition.

I would now like you to imagine the most common situations where you will need these five traits. On a separate piece of paper, list as many as you can for each trait. When you have a good list for each, choose a situation which you feel a little uneasy about and for which you need a moderate amount of improvement, preferably something coming up relatively soon. Nothing too difficult or too easy. You can work on those later after you have mastered this technique. Write that situation in column four on your Trait Anchoring worksheet. Start with only one, as I want this to be measurable. Once you have this process down, and have seen success, you can use it on as many situations as you want.

EXERCISE

Check personal ecology and congruence. Imagine yourself exemplifying this trait in the selected situation. Ask yourself these two questions: By changing the way that I respond in this situation, will this affect myself or anyone else in a negative way, and does any part of me object to making this change now? This is a critical step any time we are making any behavioral changes.

For your first situation, imagine the moment right before you will need the desired trait. Imagine it in as much detail as possible. See what you see and hear what you hear and feel what you feel.

When you feel like you have a good image, fire your

anchor and hold it. Imagine yourself exhibiting your desired trait in this situation successfully. Imagine how having this new response is going to benefit you and those around you. Feel it as intensely as you can, and when it subsides, let go of the anchor. Now break state.

Future pace. How do you experience the thought of this experience now?

Repetition, repetition, repetition. You more than likely saw some type of change in feeling toward the situation. As with any new conditioned response, you need to strengthen it. Doing something once is an action. Doing it multiple times makes it a behavior. Do it enough times and it becomes a habit.

Repeat this process for all five of your traits and all their situations.

I cannot stress enough how huge this technique can be for you moving forward. Use this. Practice this. Be your most magnificent you in as many moments as you possibly can. You don't have to wait until some future where you have prepared to become more. Become more now. You have all the power you need within you now. Be who you want to be.

CREATE YOUR IDEAL SELF

You will now create the Ideal Self you will measure your progress and growth against. Measuring progress is a key to feeling successful and happy with yourself today. As I mentioned earlier, your success is not in some far-off place or distant future. Success is not about arriving at your destination. Success is all about the quality of the journey. Your success is now and always will be now.

Your ideal self is going to be a moving target. As you change and your world changes, so will your ideals change. You may never become your ideal self. And I hope you never do. I hope your understanding of the world and your vision for your future never ceases to expand and grow. We will begin with what you have uncovered so far. You have completed quite a few worksheets that have given you a wealth of information about yourself. We will draw upon them again.

At the end of this chapter, you will find a worksheet aptly named "Your Ideal Self." There are four components to this worksheet. Four columns.

- **Column 1:** What your ideal self is not.
- **Column 2:** How you currently measure up.
- **Column 3:** What your ideal self is.
- **Column 4:** How you currently measure up.

This will give you two ways to measure your progress and feel successful now. You can see how you are moving away from your unwanted traits and how you are moving toward your ideal self. We will use this worksheet as part of your daily growth program.

WHAT YOUR IDEAL SELF IS NOT

Armed with all your worksheets in front of you, we will start by clearly establishing what your ideal self does not look like. In column one, write in all of your unwanted traits, unwanted fears, and unwanted behaviors. Write in the most glaring ones first. You can write in as many as you want to. I would recommend no more than ten for now. As you weed these out of your life you can always add more. There is a place to write in the rest of them at the end of the chapter. My first ten were dishonest, prideful, depressed, stressed, lazy, judgmental, fearful, inconsistent, gluttonous, and impatient.

HOW DO YOU MEASURE UP?

Look at each of your ten entries and ask yourself, "To what degree is this currently affecting my life?" You will measure this on a scale of one to ten with one being "this trait rarely affects your life" and ten being "it's a problem daily." Objectivity and honesty are key here.

WHAT YOUR IDEAL SELF IS

This is where you will enter your desired traits and behaviors. Begin with the ones that are the most important, then fill in the rest. Again, I would recommend no more than ten. That's plenty. Once you master some of these, you can put them on maintenance mode, and you can work on some of the others. There is a place to write in the rest of them at the end of the chapter. My first ten were honest, humble, passionate, serene, motivated, loving, kind, faith (opposite of fear), persistent/disciplined, and patient.

HOW DO YOU MEASURE UP?

Now look at each of your ten entries and ask yourself, "To what degree am I currently exhibiting this in my life?" You will measure this on a scale of one to ten, with ten being "you are very strong in this and this is a huge part of who you are," and one being "you are just developing this aspect of yourself and the only way to go is up."

This sheet you have just completed will be a huge tool for you to use daily. You are now armed with an ideal to strive towards. You know where you are and where you want to go. Chapter 8 is about taking the steps daily that will help propel you along in your journey.

You have done so much work up to this point. I know if you have done the work you have freed yourself from something that has been holding you back. Maybe it's something that has been bothering you for a great long time. I know that I had at this point, and I know you have and will continue to grow because of this work. I am humbled by it and grateful for it. I hope you are too.

In the next chapter we will get down to small daily actions that will keep you growing daily. The hard work is done. Feel good about that. It is now time to delve into the land of self mastery and life mastery. To unleash your Ideal Self on as many moments of your life as possible. You and your life are about to transform. Like a caterpillar transforming into a butterfly, it's time for you to break out and spread your wings and fly.

CHAPTER 7 KEY TAKEAWAYS

- Anyone can do anything. If it's possible and someone else has already done it, then it can be modeled and duplicated.
- You can be whoever you want to be. You can choose what character traits you want to exemplify, learn them, and wire them through anchor stacking.
- You can program yourself to respond to specific situations with these character traits by future pacing your anchors.
- Writing down what your ideal self is and isn't allows you to measure your progress and growth daily. This allows you to feel successful now.

YOUR IDEAL SELF

What my ideal self is not	How do I measure up? 1-10	What my ideal self is	How do I measure up? 1-10

REMAINING UNWANTED AND DESIRED TRAITS

Remaining Unwanted Traits	Remaining Desired Traits

CHAPTER 8

SELF MASTERY

"Before you can control conditions, you must first control yourself. Self-mastery is the hardest job you will ever tackle. If you do not conquer self, you will be conquered by self."

~ NAPOLEON HILL

I would like to share with you a metaphor that has always helped me to understand the process of growth and change you have begun and will continue to experience.

TENDING YOUR GARDEN

You have a garden that you have had for a long time, your whole life really, and have not actively been tending it. You have just decided you will do something about your garden. You have neglected it for far too long, and it is time to put some time and effort into it. Looking at your garden, there are a lot of things you need to do.

There are unwanted plants and weeds growing everywhere that need to be pulled. You want to make sure you get down deep and pull them up by the roots. The soil is not in as good a condition as it could be. You need to till it in places and pull out any rocks or unwanted roots you may have missed. Depending on the condition of it, you may need to add some limestone, or fertilizer, or mulch. Having soil that is balanced, healthy, and resilient is important for the growth of your plants.

You may have some plants and flowers and vegetables you want to keep and some that you want to add. Some of the ones that are growing are in relatively good health, while others may need some help or may need to be replanted. You want to make sure that you have all the plants you need in your garden, and you want to make sure that they have all the resources they need to grow and flourish. You want your garden to be balanced, beautiful, healthy, resilient, and productive.

Now that your garden is exactly as you want it to be, you will want to maintain it and continue to improve it and keep it beautiful. Your soil is so rich, but unfortunately, weeds and unwanted plants like rich soil just as much as your wanted plants. You will need to be diligent in pulling these weeds when they pop up. If you let them get out of control, your garden will end up how it was when you started. Or even worse, as the soil is so much healthier now.

You will notice, though, as time passes by, that the weeds are popping up less often. The plants you are growing are becoming big and strong and vibrant, and as such, need all the resources they can get. All the plants in your garden, wanted and unwanted, are vying for the same resources. It is a losing battle for the weeds, as your plants are so much stronger and healthier, and loved. You have done such a wonderful job with your garden. Moving forward, it will sustain you and bring you so much joy.

So far in this book, you have pulled out many of the weeds in your garden, or at least designated weeds and plants that need to go. You have decided which plants you want to keep and figured out which ones you would like to plant. In order to create the best garden you can, there is some work to be done. You need to pull the rest of your weeds and unwanted plants and make sure you are diligent in keeping these under control. You need to strengthen or replant the plants you want to keep and plant the ones you want to add.

PART 1: YOUR POWER OF INTENTION

We can live life in default mode and just take what life gives us, or we can be very intentional about our life and get the results that we want. The choice is ours.

Our life is an accumulation of years, months, weeks, days, hours, minutes, and moments. If we want to live the life we want to live, then we need to make sure that we are being intentional in as many moments, minutes, hours, days, weeks, months, and years as we can. In Chapter 9, "Your Life, Intentionally," we will focus on the much larger levels of intention. What we are going to focus on in this chapter is bringing our intention into every day and being aware of our intentions in as many moments as we can.

We have all had that day that started off bad and was all downhill from there. We didn't sleep well and were super tired, so we hit "snooze" a few times, which didn't help at all and may have made us more tired. When we finally got up, we felt hurried and rushed because we slept in too late. We may have spilled coffee on ourselves, stubbed our toe, or nicked ourselves shaving.

By the time we get into our car, we are not in the best frame of mind. We are super aware of how everyone is a bad driver and how overcrowded the highway is. We're a little on edge and feeling wound up and anxious. As we imagine our day at work, we see it from this state of mind: Impatient, anxious, and negative. We focus on all the things that might go wrong and the things we must do that we don't want to do. As our day progresses and our awareness is focused on these unwanted things, we seem to be attracting these unwanted things to ourselves.

When we get off work, we cannot wait to get home. What a day this has been. And then there's the traffic again. Cars everywhere. People texting or not paying attention to what they are doing. Up ahead, it looks like a few of these inattentive drivers intended to be in the same place at the same time, and that didn't work out very well for anyone, especially you. By the time you get home, you are a special kind of warped, tired, and hungry.

And then your partner asks you how your day went, and we recreate the whole thing over again, planting the seeds for a not-so-spectacular evening.

We have all had varying degrees of this kind of day. The truth is that it was all downhill from the start. This is an example of living your day in "default mode." In default mode, we take what life gives us. When we do not have a clear intention for our day, our awareness (if we want to call it that) is focused on what life is throwing at us, which leaves us in a constant state of reacting. When we choose to be intentional about our day, how we intend to believe, think, feel, and act, our awareness is focused on those things and all the opportunities throughout the day that will help us have the kind of day we intend to have.

Where your intention is, your awareness is. We have a part of our brain that is designed just for this. One function of the reticular actuating system of your brain, or RAS, is to make you aware of things that are of the greatest importance to you. Science tells us that our subconscious mind processes roughly eleven million bits of information per second from all our senses. And science also tells us that our conscious mind can only process roughly fifty bits per second. That's a huge difference. Some studies have found the difference to be even larger. Your RAS helps you to focus on the fifty bits of information per second that are of the greatest importance to you. There is an abundance of books and papers and studies that expand upon this science. This is not one of those books. For the purpose of this book, all that is necessary is to understand how to use it to your advantage. You are not learning the physics behind electricity and light. You are learning how to flip the light switch.

Here are a few examples of this process in action.

Visual. Have you ever been shopping for a specific model, color, or type of car and began to see those models and that color of car and that type of car everywhere? Or, if you have ever been in the market for a home or apartment, you become aware of "for sale" signs and "now renting" signs.

Auditory. A mother isolating the voice of her child in a busy playground. Or, you are at a party talking with some friends, and through all the noise, you hear your name spoken from the other side of the room, and your awareness automatically snaps in that direction.

Kinesthetic. Have you ever stubbed your toe and become very aware that it is there? Were you consciously aware of your toe before you stubbed it? When was the last time you were consciously aware of your toe? Or your eyebrows? Or the feeling of air moving through your nose as you breathe? Have you ever been hungry and suddenly you were acutely aware of the food in whatever show you are watching, or keyed in on someone talking about food, or become extra aware of any food smells nearby?

An exercise to illustrate how the RAS works.

Exercise 1: For the next thirty seconds, count as many red objects as you can. It can be anything. Even if something only has a speck of red on it, count it.

Exercise 2: Turn on your TV and pick any show. For the next five minutes, count how often people say the word "I."

- How many red objects did you count in Exercise 1?
- How many times did you hear the word "I" in Exercise 2?
- Now, how many white objects did you see during Exercise 1?
- Now, how often did someone say someone else's name in Exercise 2?

You were not made aware of the white objects or other people's names, as they weren't of importance to you. You had only fifty bits per second to process, so you were made aware of the things you intentionally set out to count. What this exercise illustrates is that if you feel as if something is not important to you, you will not be fully aware of it happening.

PART 2: SETTING YOUR INTENTION

What you will be learning in Part 2 is how to set your intention daily, so you can break free from default-mode living and live the life you want to live.

Every time we wake up in the morning, we are embarking upon a new day. To repeat, every time we wake up in the morning, we are embarking on a new day. When I woke up this morning, today was a new day. Yesterday did not exist anymore, including all the good things and bad things I did. None of my beliefs, emotions, thoughts, or the behaviors I exhibited yesterday are true for me when I wake up, at least not yet.

Wanted or unwanted, for them to be in this day, I need to bring them into this day, and that happens right away. As we have discovered, most of our beliefs, emotions, thoughts, fears, and behaviors are automatic and are a function of our subconscious mind. We know how powerful the subconscious mind is. Our subconscious mind likes routine, and fears change. Our subconscious mind likes default mode. It knows that the life you have created for yourself has not killed you, and your subconscious is ok with more of the same. But your subconscious mind is something that you have the power to program.

If we do not consciously and intentionally give our subconscious mind instructions on what we want it to focus on today, then more of the same is exactly what we can expect. And that might be ok if we don't have a bunch of fires to put out in our life right now. We can coast through today and be ok. And then a month passes by. And then a year. And then a decade. This is the inertia of our life. The thing to remember is the key point of this book. If nothing changes, then nothing changes. 1 + 1 will never equal 3.

Right when we wake up and right before we go to bed are the best times to give our subconscious mind instructions.

During this window, we see an overlap of our conscious and subconscious minds. At this time, our subconscious mind is open to suggestions. So right when you wake up, before the default mode gets a hold of you, is the best time to set your intentions for the day. And that is what you will be doing in Part 3.

PART 3: CREATING YOUR MORNING PROGRAM
It is my hope that you see the importance of starting your day off intentionally and the opportunity for growth it holds for you. Please be patient with yourself. As with any new skill or habit, it will take time to develop and strengthen. There is no such thing as a perfect day. By setting your intentions daily though, you are setting yourself up for success, learning to live your life on purpose, and choosing not to just settle for whatever life gives you.

I chose the word "program" over more commonly used words like "routine" or "ritual" or "activities" because the word "program" speaks more to what we are doing. We are programming our minds as to how we want to show up today and what is important for us to be aware of today.

DESIRED TRAITS
So, what does a good morning program look like? At the end of Part 3, I have included your Daily Success Program worksheet so you can put this all together. Pull out the Your Ideal Self sheet you created and look at your desired traits. The only way these traits will manifest in your life is if you actually choose to use them in your life. The practice we are doing to "wire" these traits into us is good and necessary, but nothing ever happens if we don't get in the game and use them. I recommend you include all ten of the desired traits in your

morning routine. You want to be aware of opportunities to use these new and improved responses to life. You will be beginning your day with an intention to live this day in accordance with your highest ideal.

I have all my desired traits written on the unlined side of a three-by-five card. One trait per card. On the lined side, I have written down examples of me exhibiting this trait in my life. So, if the desired trait is confidence, I would remember times when I was confident. This makes it easier for me to reassociate with the desired trait. I just remember that time in as much detail as I can, especially the emotional, postural, and breathing components of it. I also have many modeling examples of other people embodying these traits. So, in the example of confidence, I write down people that are confident. I also write down any common submodalities. For example, if in all the examples of confidence, there is a common posture or breathing, or there is a common physical sensation somewhere in my body, or if there are any common visual or auditory aspects to it. I write these down in as abbreviated a way as I can. Every time I intend one of these traits for the day, I take the time to read what I have written down, and I practice that state at that moment.

The key is to not just say the trait out loud or think it, but to take thirty seconds or so to really embody the desired trait as much as you possibly can in any way you can. Feel what it feels like. See yourself exhibiting this trait. Hear yourself say the trait out loud.

I do not like to include negatives in my morning routine for an important reason. Our subconscious does not understand the concept of "no" or "don't want." So, if I said, "I don't want to be impatient today," all my subconscious hears is "I want to be impatient today." If you have any unwanted traits you need to work on, intend the opposite. For example, "I am patient today" as opposed to "I don't want to be impatient today." Or "I am calm and serene in traffic today" as opposed to "I am not going to freak out and road rage in traffic today."

DESIRED AWARENESS

This is where we intend the things we want to be made aware of. As an example, maybe we are stalled in a business project and are having a hard time figuring out the best way to proceed. We could intend, "Today, I am aware of all the opportunities that present themselves, from all sources and in all forms, to successfully move this project forward."

Or maybe we have an important decision to make and are having difficulty figuring out the best way to go. We could intend, "Today I am aware of all the knowledge, wisdom, and insight, from all sources and in all forms, that will help me make the best decision in this matter."

Or maybe we have financial goals that we have set, but we don't have the slightest idea as to how we will get there. We might intend, "Today I am aware of and open-minded to all the inspiration, ideas, and methods presented to me today, from all sources and in all forms, that will help me develop a plan to reach this financial goal."

Notice the "from all sources and in all forms." When tasking the subconscious with finding a solution, we need to be open to all potential sources of insight, insight that may come in all forms. We never know what form it will come from. Someone might be talking about something having nothing to do with your intention, but a word or a phrase or how they are talking or their body language will trigger something in your mind that will lead you to the answer you seek. Or you might be flipping through channels and feel the need, or a "tug," to pause and back up and not know why. And you'll find someone is speaking about something related to what you have intended. Or maybe something seemingly unwanted will happen, but you act out of character and are unusually calm. Being calm, you see that hidden within this unwanted event there is insight or inspiration having nothing to do with the event itself that points you in the direction you need to go. Something you wouldn't have normally learned of had you reacted as you normally would.

Remember, when doing this in the morning, we are, to one degree or another, leveraging the power of our subconscious mind. Our subconscious mind that can process eleven million bits of information per second. When we keep an open mind to "all sources and all forms," we develop our sense of intuition and become open to receive inspiration. This is a sense that will grow over time.

DESIRED FOCUS

This is where you will set your intention for things you would like to accomplish today. These will be things like, "I completed the sixth chapter of my book today" or "I finished pulling all the weeds in my garden today" or "I had a transformational coaching session with one of my clients today" or "I summoned the courage to ask for a raise today."

We need to be somewhat realistic with these. Our subconscious mind needs to feel like it is possible. If it does not think it's possible (if you don't believe it's possible), your mind will resist it. Remember, our subconscious wants to keep us safe, and if we fail, our security may be threatened. You must crawl before you walk and walk before you run. As time goes on, though, and your belief in your abilities grows, you will start intending to achieve things out of your comfort zone. Things you have details on but do not have the slightest idea about how to put it all together. You will intend it though because you believe in the power of your subconscious mind, or you believe in the power of your God. That is where things get really good. You will look at things you do not understand, things that used to make you nervous, and say to yourself, "I got this. I can do this. Consider it done."

Now that you have some ideas of what types of intentions you can set for the day, let's pull it all together and learn how to best execute your program. Turn to the end of this chapter and look at your Daily Success Program worksheet. Make a bunch of copies of this, as you will change it daily. Or you can just use a notebook. I did this for the longest time, and it works great.

The worksheet is simple. You have a column for the traits you want to strengthen, things you want to be aware of, and things you want to accomplish. As a part of your Evening Program, you will fill this sheet out so it will be ready for you when you wake up. All you have to do in the morning is get up and do it.

A key thing to remember when doing this is that the most effective way to wire our subconscious mind is through intense and richly detailed visualization. The mind cannot distinguish between real or imagined phenomena. When you say an intention out loud it is considered an affirmation. When you add to it a visual aspect, emotion, and belief it has happened, then it becomes something altogether more powerful. There is nothing wrong with affirmations. I use them in all types of different ways. To get the full effect, though, your subconscious needs to believe this intention is real.

The three keys to setting your intention are:

- **Having a visual, auditory, and a powerful kinesthetic/feeling component to it.**
- **Believing that the experience you present to your subconscious is real and true. Try to act as if you are remembering it happening.**
- **Bringing as much energy as you can to the kinesthetic quality of the experience**.

In Chapter 7, you completed an anchor-stacking exercise. Using these anchors in this situation can make the intentions that much stronger. In that exercise and throughout this book, you have learned to put together experiences with visual, auditory, and kinesthetic/feeling components. You have learned how to intensify them. The more you practice this skill, the better you will get at it and the easier it will become. A lot of these intentions you will reuse often, and as such they will become stronger and easier every time you set them.

For each of your intentions, as you are saying them out loud, see what you would see and feel what you would feel having successfully realized that intention for the day. Make it as real and intense as you can. Each one should take about thirty seconds, just long enough for the intention to create a feeling within you. Go through all of these in succession until they are all done. At the end of your morning program, you can feel a broad range of emotions depending on the day and the intensity of the practice, and how well you slept the night before.

These include feelings of positive expectation, inspiration, passion, joy, love, gratitude, or humility. It can be anything, really. Sometimes I feel so fired up I could wrestle a bear or run out into traffic and tackle a car. Some days I am left with a feeling of neutrality or peace and calm. It varies; and no matter how you feel, it's ok.

Consistency is critical with this, and that's why we always want to keep this simple, especially in the beginning. You want to do it long enough to see some positive results and make it a strong habit, like taking a shower and brushing your teeth.

MY MORNING PROGRAM FOR TODAY

I would now like to share with you my morning intentions program from today. I have been doing some type of daily success program for the past ten years, so there is an intuitive quality to it. I will have a structured morning program from the night before, but my intuition will have me change my intentions to something else. Sometimes I fall short of the ideal and don't do a great morning program. I am by no means perfect. I do the best I can. I can tell you, though, that when I do this consistently, I create all types of growth and momentum in my life.

This morning I woke up at 3:00am. I was super tired. I worked my intentions almost immediately and realized they were garbage. They had no life to them. I had to find some energy. I turned to my "Morning Motivation" playlist to infuse a little energy into my morning. About five minutes into "Free Bird" by Lynyrd Skynyrd, I had found my energy and felt like I could run through a wall and eat my neighbor's breakfast. I settled back into my intentions. They were really simple.

- "I am impeccable in my word today. Everything that comes out of my mouth today is positive and true."
- "God and I have written Chapter 8 and it was better than I ever hoped it could be."

- "I am a channel of God's love and light today."
- "I walk in faith today, knowing that my spirit and God will guide me."
- "All the material things I need today are provided for me."
- "My motives are pure today."

At some point in there I fired my omega anchor, increased it, and reset it. At this point, I was feeling pretty fired up. Maybe a little too so. Feeling the need to come down out of the clouds a bit and put my feet on the ground, I did a Surrender Prayer/Meditation. I am a very spiritual person. I feel that when I am running the show with my lower self, or my ego, the results can vary. I know that when I surrender the "how" to my higher faculties (subconscious and spirit), the results I get are better than I ever could have imagined and are usually in better harmony with the greater good. I set my timer on my phone for ten minutes. My surrender prayer is a simple expression of gratitude for all that has been given to me, followed by the question, "What would you have me be today?" I then meditate and wait patiently and humbly for the answer.

The next thing I did was a gratitude and love list. This is simple. I set my timer on my phone for five minutes. I spend about half the time writing down everything I am grateful for. I write it down on a piece of paper (I have a gratitude and love list journal), say it out loud with a feeling of gratitude in my heart, and say "thank you." I spend the second half of the five minutes writing down the people in my life I love. I try to allow them to naturally present themselves. For instance, my dad may pop into my mind. I say, "I love you, Dad," and smile. I will see him in my mind's eye, imagine where he is on the planet at that moment, and quickly imagine him filled with love and light. By then, someone else has usually popped into my mind and I begin to love them.

Sometimes I love a whole family at the same time. This morning I brought my brother and his family into my heart all at the same time. I do that for the rest of the five minutes. The feeling of love and gratitude in my heart when this is done is hard to explain. Tears of joy often wet my face during this activity, as they do right now as I am writing about it.

The next thing I did was a Love and Light Meditation for ten minutes. I begin with where I am sitting and imagine a wave of love and light flowing out of me in all directions. When I cannot see the front of the wave any longer, I pull myself up and out of my body and view it from a higher vantage point. Usually well up above the earth. I imagined this wave flowing across the Pacific, loving, and blessing all the creatures of the sea, and I saw it pour across Asia and down over Australia and all the islands I saw giant lights by the coast, which I imagined to be cities full of people. The wave then poured over the Middle East, up over Europe, down the African continent, and across the Atlantic to South America and up over North America. There was so much love there. The animals in the Serengeti made themselves readily apparent. The wave went up over Europe and came down over North America and South America. Pulling back even further still, I saw the entire Earth enveloped in love and light. It felt like it was one giant being. I pulled that image of the Earth into my body where my heart was and just felt the love. This is different every time. I just focus on the expansion of love and light.

I then spent ten minutes strengthening my omega anchor. (You will create your own omega anchor later in Part 2 of this book.) Some people add exercise, yoga, or breathwork to their morning program. I will often do future-self meditations, which we will discuss in detail later in this book.

The key to your initial success with this program will be to keep it simple. Just set your intentions consistently every morning and make it a strong habit, then you can add things in. Focus on increasing the quality and intensity of your intentions. The intentions should take only ten minutes, tops. If you commit to ten minutes per morning for the next month, you will see dramatic positive changes in yourself and your quality of life. I challenge you to do this now. Take ten minutes and go through your intentions now. Write them down and go for it. At the very least, prepare your intentions for tomorrow morning. Do it again the next day. And the next day. Put yourself and your life on notice. This is how it will be from now on. Communicate it with all that you have ever been, are, and ever will be.

PART 4: CREATING YOUR EVENING PROGRAM
The evening program is all about increasing your awareness of everything having to do with you. It allows you to feel the joy that comes from acknowledging your progress and growth. It is about bringing in as many positives as you can into your night's rest, and for preparing your intentions for the following morning.

You will be using your Daily Success Program worksheet for this. The evening program section is an evaluation of how you measured up today to your unwanted traits and ideal traits as well as a list of any other successes of the day. This produces a self-mastery feedback loop. I have my Ideal Self sheet out every time I do my evening program.

Column one is for your unwanted traits. Referring to

your Ideal Self sheet, starting with your unwanted traits, ask yourself this question for each trait, "Did I at any point today exhibit this trait?" If you answered yes to any of them, write them down in column one. Think about how you would like to act the next time a similar situation occurs. Do not beat yourself up. Take whatever good is in it and let go of the rest. This is how we grow as human beings. We are not supposed to be perfect.

Column two is for your ideal traits. Ask yourself the same question. "Did I at any point today exhibit this trait?" If the answer is yes, add it to column two. Allow yourself to feel good about this as well. Now look at the ones that were a "no." Ask yourself if there were any opportunities today where you could have exhibited these traits.

In column three, celebrate any successes you had today. What happened that was good? What did you do today that you can be proud of? Allow yourself to write down anything that comes to your mind you can feel good about. Celebrate your successes every day. This is huge for self-esteem, self-confidence, self-worth, and increasing your quality of life. Celebrating our successes every day helps build positive momentum in our lives.

At the very bottom of your sheet is an especially important question: "Do I owe any amends to anyone?" If the answer is "yes," write it down and decide what you need to do, if anything, to make that right tomorrow (if it cannot get handled today). If so, put that on your intention sheet for tomorrow.

Before you set your evening program down, take a minute to look at it in its totality. See if anything jumps out at you. If you are looking at your day objectively and honestly, you should see that the number of positive things you did today far outnumbers the negative things today. This whole exercise should take around ten minutes at the most, unless there is some profound reflection going on, which is totally awesome. That is the good stuff.

By working these programs diligently and consistently, you will notice that your awareness of how you are reacting or responding during the day is increasing. You will find that your ability to insert a pause between an event and your response is increasing. Your ability to deal with others will get better and better every day. What they do and how they think and how they feel will affect you less and less. You will become aware of your thoughts and decide whether they are true for you or not. And if they are not, simply love them and let them go. This will give you greater control over your emotions. Instead of every thought getting through and triggering the corresponding emotional response, you will filter those unwanted thoughts out before they ever get to your emotions. You will notice that your emotional nature becomes much more balanced. As the fearful thoughts become fewer and fewer, and your negative emotions are triggered less and less, a space will open up within you. This space, which used to be filled with fear and pain, will now be filled with feelings of peace, serenity, and joy.

This is the life I live today. I have seen these results manifest in countless individuals. I have seen lives that were completely ruined, rebuilt upon a firm foundation. I have witnessed people transformed, seemingly reborn in every possible way. I have seen these people live wonderful, fulfilling, successful, and prosperous lives. They will tell you that the life they live today is better than anything they ever thought was possible. It was difficult at times, and still can be difficult at times. Life does not stop happening all around us. Life will always be "lifey." As we continue to grow, our understanding and ability to consciously define what life means, and how we allow it to affect us, grows.

Every one of these people and I have one thing in common. We put in the work. We grabbed onto a plan that worked, and we worked it. We persisted. We persevered. Day by day, step by step, moment by moment. You too will create these results in your life. Be willing to do the work. Be willing to overcome. Be willing to see this through. This is the path to the ideal. This is the path to self mastery.

The sole purpose of writing this book was to help others feel the peace and joy and love that is in my heart on a daily basis. The only way we truly keep these gifts is by giving them away. I hope if there was something impactful in this book so far that you choose to share it with someone else. In doing so you help that individual, and you will strengthen it in yourself.

You are well on your way, fellow traveler. You've done so much and come so far. I am so very grateful you have taken the time to read this book up to this point. It means that you have improved yourself and your life. You have found moments of peace and joy and love that you might not have found otherwise.

In Part 2 of this book, you will become the master of your life. In a way you already have. The first words of introduction to this book are:

"Life doesn't give us what we want. It gives us what we are. If we want our lives to change, we need to change ourselves. If we want something different, then we must be willing to be different. If we want more, we must first become more."

CHAPTER 8 KEY TAKEAWAYS

- We can leave our days on default mode, or we can program our subconscious with our intentions for the day.

- The more sensory detail we put into our intentions for the day, (Visualize the intentions as being done. Feel like you are there, accomplishing the intention with all the emotional intensity you can. Speak the words out loud), the more powerful they become.

- Take ten minutes at night and ten minutes in the morning for the next thirty days. Do this and you will see remarkable positive changes in yourself and your life.

DAILY SUCCESS PROGRAM WORKSHEET

Date:	Evening Program	
Unwanted Traits	Ideal Traits	Misc. Successes
Do I owe amends to anyone?		

Date:	Tomorrow Morning's Intentions	
Intended Character Traits	Intended Awareness	Intended Goal Focus

PART TWO

MASTER YOUR LIFE

CHAPTER 9

YOUR LIFE INTENTIONALLY

"Dream lofty dreams, and as you dream, so you shall become. Your vision is the promise of what you shall one day be; your ideal is the prophecy of what you shall at last unveil."

~JAMES ALLEN

Your life will happen, whether you're ready for it or not. Your life is happening right now. We've all said or heard people say, "Wow! That month flew by so fast!" or "I can't believe it's been a whole year!" or even more seriously, "They grow up so fast. Where did all the time go? I wish I would have spent more time with them." Or even a bit more seriously, "I can't believe this is the end. There are so many things I wish I had done." I know that last one is a bit morbid, but there is someone, somewhere, saying that right now, feeling the feeling of regret that must come with ending one's life on that note.

We will all die. No one gets out of this thing alive. What will you do with the time you have left? If someone told you that you had only a year to live, how would you spend that year? What would be important to you? What would your priorities be? I know. It's a super serious line of questioning. Serious, yet necessary.

Allow these questions to sink in while I share with you one of my own personal experiences on this matter. My father's father had one of the biggest positive influences on me of anyone in my life. When I was seventeen years old, I was in all types of trouble. I could not hold a job. Could not pay my bills. Hooked on drugs. Just altogether lost in every way. One month, I asked my grandparents if they would loan me some money so I could pay my rent. They declined but offered me a job at an apartment complex they managed. My grandmother Hazel ran the front office while my grandpa Ike handled all the maintenance and landscaping.

When I started work there, my job was to help my grandfather with landscaping and general repairs. What I learned, quickly, was that I had no idea what hard work was. See, my grandfather grew up on a farm, and it seems like things were a little bit more labor-intensive in those days. My grandfather's low gear was my high gear. Sometimes, I had to take a break, but he just kept going. Working with my grandfather for that month changed my life in so many ways. He showed me what hard work was. His whole countenance and character seemed to rub off on me. He instilled in me a strong work ethic. When I started work there, I was unsure of myself, lost, and did not know how to do this thing called "life" that seemed so difficult and daunting to a seventeen-year-old boy. What I learned from my grandfather's example was that if I worked hard, and did the right thing, that everything would be ok.

I had an eighth-grade education and no prospects. But I worked hard, and in doing so, I built a good life for myself. I had a successful career in the automobile industry. I was extremely proud of the fact that I had succeeded in life to the extent that I had. To have come as far as I had.

One job I had was quite a commute for me, but it passed by my grandma and grandpa's house. The first week I worked there, I stopped over at my grandparent's house before I went home. It was great. I could hang out with them, maybe watch a ball game on TV, Grandma would fix me some grub, and I could wait until traffic died down before going home. I told them I would do this regularly, and they were super excited about that. But for the next year, I would hear my grandma say, "We love you, Kyle. We sure would like you to stop by one day." Or I would hear my grandfather say, "I love you, Kyle. Hope to see you soon." I can hear their voices now like it was yesterday. See, it wasn't that I was too busy or didn't want to see them. I figured I would just do it tomorrow. Or next week. I'd do it some other day.

And then my grandfather passed away. I was devastated. He was such an important part of me. I felt so guilty. I always thought there would be more time. I would have given anything to see him one last time and tell him what he meant and how much I loved him. My grandmother said that he knew how I felt, and I believe that. But that did not stop me from crucifying myself for it.

I carried this with me for a great long time. I drank at that regret and guilt on many occasions. The first time I did the Personal Inventory you did in Chapter 4, he was one person I needed to make amends to. I needed to forgive myself but did not know how. I made a living amends by taking my grandma to church like he used to. As I walked with my grandma, ever so slowly toward the front door of the church, I felt him with me. As I sat in church those many Sundays, I was able to forgive myself.

See, sometimes there is not a tomorrow or a next week or some other time. It is so easy to get caught up in life and take for granted things we should never take for granted. We get caught up by the inertia of our life, and years and decades pass. Tomorrow never happens. By taking the time to discover what is important to you, and prioritizing those things in your life, you will never have to regret not doing something ever again.

YOUR JOURNEY BEGINS HERE
We spoke a lot about the difference between settling for whatever life gives us and being intentional about our lives. In Chapter 8, you learned to begin your day by setting your intentions for that day. This is a remarkably simple activity to do, yet there is something magical that happens when we apply it to our lives. This chapter is about applying this activity to your life.

You can realize that you are not where you want to be, and decide where you want to go, but until you take that first step toward it, nothing will happen. I am not happy with where I am at with myself and my life, yet today, I choose to do the same things I did yesterday. That is just a recipe for more of the same. That is the definition of insanity.

It's time to take some of that power you freed up from your past, and from all the energy that comes with not being ok with one's self and past, and begin applying it to changing your circumstances and situations in life. It is time to become the master of your life, the author of the book that is your existence, the architect of all the beauty you plan on building. It is time. You have all the power within you. Now let's do what it takes to draw it out and apply it.

At the end of this chapter I have provided a Your Journey Begins Here worksheet. This will clearly show you where you are and where you want to go.

TWO PINS IN THE MAP WORKSHEET

Area of your life	Where are you currently on a scale of 1-10	Where you are going	Potential Synergy

PUTTING PINS IN THE MAP
STEP 1: DEFINING THE TERRITORY

What you will do now is list all the areas in your life you want to develop. These can be any areas you feel are important to you. I will give you examples so you get an idea of what to look for, but make this 100% about what is important to you. Not what you think you should do because everyone else does, but what deep down inside, behind all your fears, you know is important to you.

Examples would be self mastery, knowledge/education, career, finances, romantic relationships, family and friends, material environment (homes, cars, food, toys), spiritual development, health, personal well-being, personal achievements (completing an Iron Man, climbing a mountain, writing a book), or community (charity, service, politics, religion). You can put anything down that you want to. When you decide what is important to you and what you would like to change and improve, write those things down in column 1 of your Pins in the Map worksheet on the previous page.

STEP 2: WHERE YOU ARE

Step 2 is about getting a general sense of where you are currently so you can get an idea of how far you need to go. Gauge how you are showing up in these categories on a scale of 1-10; "1" being that it is as far away from the ideal as possible, and "10" being you have accomplished your ideal. Be objective here. You want to give yourself an honest appraisal. Otherwise, the only person you are deceiving is yourself.

One thing to consider when appraising these areas is the amount of time and effort required to reach your ideal. Consider how much time and effort you think would get from where you are to where you want to go. Things like, I need to get an eight-year degree, or I need to lose fifty pounds and run a marathon but have never run five miles before. Or it might take a short amount of time, or no time. I can improve the quality of my relationships with my friends and family in a short time by just switching priorities around and spending more time with them and choosing to care more about them. I believe anything is possible, but we also need to remember that Rome was not built in a day. This is being objective. This is being honest. Again, in this chapter, we are not digging into these topics in great depth. That will happen later. What we are looking for is a general sense of direction and scope.

STEP 3: WHERE YOU ARE GOING
You will now define your ideal for each area. You will not be getting into exact details, or how you will get there, in this chapter. That will happen later. What we are looking for here is a general answer to the following question.

If you knew this area of your life could be any way you want it to be, what would that look like?

Take your time to allow this ideal to come to the surface. You might refer back to what you came up with in Chapter 1.

I know sometimes it's hard to do the whole "If you knew you could not fail, what would you do?" exercise and buy into it completely and wholeheartedly. What I want you to start believing is if someone else can do it, then so can you. That if it has been proven to be possible, that you can do it.

All practical considerations aside, allow yourself to dream. Allow yourself to get a little uncomfortable and stretch your belief of what is possible. Remember, at one point in human history, creating tools was all the rage, and to think that we could create and harness the power of fire was just crazy talk. And don't get our unevolved ancestors started on language. "Writing? Books? That's just insane!" At one point, the earth was at the center of the universe. All the planets and stars revolved around us (no false pride happening there), and to speak otherwise might have gotten you in big trouble. Just ask Galileo. At one point, the earth was flat. If you sailed too far, you would fall off the edge of it and get eaten by giant sea or space monsters (not sure what you would call those pesky monsters). At one point, the thought of an airplane was lunacy, and people that thought it was possible were ostracized and considered foolish and crazy, yet we found a way to put a man on the moon. At one point, we had no electricity. At one point, we had no cell phones. At one point, a human could not run a mile in under four minutes. Then Roger Bannister did it and suddenly, many people have done it that it's not that big of a deal anymore. I could go on and on and on.

What I am trying to get at is there is a first time for everything. I believe that anything is possible. The only thing that limits our own evolution is ourselves. The human potential is limitless. Miracles do happen, and they are happening around us every single day. So allow yourself to dream a little.

When you have a good idea of what you want, take the time to experience it in as much detail as you can. Like you have done so often in this book, see what you would see, hear what you would hear, feel what you would feel, as if you were experiencing this ideal now. Test-drive it if you will. Make sure it feels right. We will be doing an exercise later that will help you consider this in much greater detail. For now, if it feels right, write it down in column three.

STEP 4: PRIORITIZING YOUR JOURNEYS

You now know where you are, where you want to go, and how far you will need to go. Step 4 is about how each area affects each other and how much each contributes to the quality of your life. In this step, we are looking for a better understanding of where we should focus our time and effort.

Now consider column three, where you want to go. Go through each one and ask yourself, "Does this enhance any of the other areas of my life?" What you are looking for is opportunities for synergy. Synergy is where focusing on one area will help another area, and how those two improvements will help one another. This is the idea that the whole is greater than the sum of its parts. You are looking for ways to maximize your return on your most precious commodity, which is all the moments of your life moving forward.

An example of potential synergy would be investing time and effort to increase your education, which enhances career development, which can enhance your finances, material environment, romantic relationships, community, and personal achievements, etc.

Another example of potential synergy would be health. By investing time in and increasing your level of health, you help all the other areas of your life. You have more energy and better focus for your education and career, which enhances your finances, which, as we already know, helps a lot of other areas. Better health will enhance your romantic relationships, family and friends, personal achievements, community, and spiritual development.

In column four, write what areas would be enhanced by you spending time in this area.

Take a second here to consider what you have done so far. You have logically and sensibly looked at this from a variety of angles. Now disregard logic and sense and reason. Just throw it all out the window. Now listen to your heart. Look at each area of your life and allow yourself to understand what is most important at this point in your life. Don't worry if it doesn't make any sense at all. Sometimes what "makes sense" is a limit placed upon us by society. Sometimes our heart wants what it wants for a reason. Allow yourself to consider these questions.

- "What are you passionate about?"
- "What will you not compromise for any reason whatsoever?"
- "What have you always wanted to do or always wanted to be?"

The only thing left to do is rank the areas of your life from most important to least important. Knowing what you value most in life will help you make important decisions in your life. What you value will change over time as you change. What you have done so far will allow you to make a good beginning.

PREPARE FOR YOUR JOURNEY

You have a general sense of what you want your life to look like and how you would like those areas to develop and grow. Preparing for your journey is about looking at your ideals for each area of your life and discovering the quality of person you need to become for you to reach your ideal in each area. Your life results from your past traits, thoughts, and behaviors, etc. What traits, thoughts, and behaviors does a person excelling in those areas possess? In Part 1 of this book, you did extensive work in establishing your ideal self. What you will do now is compare your ideal self and your ideal life, see where you may need to adjust, and gain more understanding of which of your traits will lend themselves to achieving your ideal in each area of your life.

MODELING

What you will be doing in this exercise is creating a model of the qualities you will need to embody to reach your ideal for each area of your life. Have your Ideal Self sheet ready, as you will be referring to it in this exercise.

Step 1: Take your life areas in order of importance and write them in the first column of the Your Journey Begins Here worksheet at the end of the chapter.

Step 2: For each area of your life, list all the traits and skills you have that will help you to achieve your ideal in this category. Write those down in column two.

Step 3: For each area, come up with three people you admire that are already living up to your ideal in this area. It's ok if you can't think of three. Just do your best. Write these in column three.

Step 4: Take your time with this one. Imagine each person, with as much detail as possible, successfully embodying your ideal in this area.

- Imagine what they look like.
- Where are they at?
- What are they wearing?
- What is their hair like?
- What are they saying?
- What are their facial expressions like?
- Are they moving?

When you have built a good image of them, lift up out of your body and settle down into theirs. See what they see. Hear what they hear. Feel what they feel. Now that you are as associated with this person as you can be, ask yourself these three questions.

- "What character traits do they have that are helping them succeed in this area?"
- "What behaviors or habits do they have that are helping them succeed in this area?"
- "What specialized skills and knowledge do they have that is helping them succeed in this area?"

Write the answer to these questions in column four.

Step 5: Now, ask yourself these questions:

- "What traits, behaviors, habits, skills, or knowledge do they have that I do not currently possess or have but need to develop further?"
- "Are there any other traits, behaviors, habits, skills, or knowledge I do not have that will help me reach my ideal in this area?"

Write all the answers to these questions in column five.
Step 6: Now, look at your ideal for each area of your life. Ask yourself,

- "What has been holding me back thus far?"
- "What have been some obstacles I have not overcome yet?"

These can include things like external factors, you haven't really attempted to improve it yet, you haven't prioritized the time, physical limitations, people holding you back, lack of education, limiting beliefs, fear, etc; anything that you can think of that you feel has limited or obstructed your progress. Write your answers to these questions in column six.

By modeling someone, we are applying their template or their recipe for success to our own life. Sometimes parts of the recipe are missing. This is not something to get upset about or down on yourself about, nor should you allow what you don't know yet to get you down or deter you from moving forward. If you are trying to bake a cake and are missing a couple of eggs, then just go to the store and get the eggs. It's that simple. All that is needed is planning and action. There is no magic involved. Someone else has baked that cake before, and so will you.

This chapter has clarified where you currently are, where you want to go, and how long it will take you to get there. You have examined each area of your life and are beginning to realize what is most important in your life. This is a huge realization. A person cannot live their life with true intention if they are not clear on what they want. The rest of this book will help you to become crystal clear on what you want, so clear that it may almost seem as though it already happened.

As you move into the life mastery portion of this book, remember that life will give you what you are, not what you want. The quality of your life will not grow if you do not continue to grow yourself. Being diligent with your daily success and growth routine is the most important thing you can do to increase the quality of your life. Let me repeat that. Being diligent with your daily success and growth routine is the most important thing you can do to increase the quality of your life. This is something you can control. You are in complete control of yourself and your life. You got this.

CHAPTER 9 KEY TAKEAWAYS

- As with our personal growth, our life will not become better if we do not intend it to do so. We might luck out and have things go our way, but until we figure out what we want and intend to get it, all we will get is more of what we have been getting.

- If one person can do something, then so can you. You might need to change, and learn, and grow, but if the task is a possibility, you can learn how to do it successfully.

- Modeling is a method of duplicating the methods that someone else used to achieve an outcome you would like to achieve. It is their recipe for success. Follow the directions and achieve the same outcome.

YOUR JOURNEY BEGINS HERE WORKSHEET

						Area of your Life
						Your current supporting traits and skills
						People successful in this area you want to model
						Their supporting traits and skills
						Area-specific traits and skills you must develop
						Obstacles

CHAPTER 10

PLAN YOUR WORK

"If one advances confidently in the direction of his dreams, and endeavors to live the life which he has imagined, he will meet with a success unexpected in common hours."

~ HENRY DAVID THOREAU

Chapter 9 armed you with a good sense of how you want your life to unfold moving forward. A general sense is a good beginning. It is an excellent framework, but for these things to happen in your life, you need to get as specific as you can about three things. These will be the three parts of this chapter.

What you want specifically.
Why you really want it.
How you intend to get it.

PART 1: WHAT YOU WANT SPECIFICALLY

Understanding the difference between a general and a specific goal is important. A general goal is not actually a goal at all. General goals like, "I just want to be happy," or, "I want to be as successful as I can," are not actually goals at all. Wanting to be happy and successful is a good thing, and a necessary thing. Things like "I want to feel loved," or "I want to feel secure financially," or "I want a more rewarding job" are all great. One who says these things might feel like they know what they want. Unfortunately, if they stop there, they will still be at the mercy of life and what it gives them. They need to take more steps.

They need to ask themselves questions like, "How do I know when I feel happy? What is it in my life that has made me feel happy? What do I think might make me happy in the future?"

Or "How will I know when I'm financially secure? What does that feel like? What would the circumstances need to be for me to feel financially secure?"

Or "What is it that's not rewarding about my current job? What would my next job have to be like for me to feel rewarded in it? How will I know when to feel like I am rewarded?"

We need to refine it down for these things to happen in our lives. Again, we can wait and hope that life will give us the life we want, or we can choose to intentionally live the life we want to live.

Looking at your "Two Pins in the Map worksheet" from Chapter 9, you may be specific on some things, while others still need refinement. You will now go through each area of your life and define one goal you feel will dramatically improve that area of your life. I know that you may have more goals in that area, and the goals you achieve will more than likely lead to other bigger goals. Let's start with just one for now. How would you feel if you improved every area of your life? What would that be like? What will your future look like from that vantage point?

CREATE A WELL-DEFINED GOAL

The first thing you want to do is write in all the areas of your life by level of importance in column one of the What and Why worksheet at the end of this chapter.

For a goal to be well-defined, it must contain two key elements. It must be specific and it must be time sensitive. You must know precisely what it is, and it has to have a specific date for it to be achieved by. A lot of schools of thought require more elements to have a well-defined goal. I want to keep this simple. What you will do and when will you have it done by. Simple.

The first thing you will do is get specific on what you want to accomplish in each area of your life. Turn again to your list of the areas you are working on. Take your most important area and allow yourself to write down every specific goal or achievement or action you believe would help you improve in this area of your life. You may already know what you want in this area of your life. And that is ok. Put that down too. This is a brainstorming exercise. Let the words flow. When they stop, wait a minute. Stop thinking about it, then turn back to it again. Continue to not think at all. Don't focus on any one thing. Allow yourself to look at all of it. You want to allow your intuition time to show you something. You want to allow time for inspiration to slip in. Just look at all the items on your sheet for a minute or two. When you believe you have defined what you want in this area, run it past the two criteria for a well-defined goal.

IS IT SPECIFIC?

Making millions of dollars is not specific. Making 1.2 million dollars would be specific. Getting in the best shape of your life is not specific. Running five miles in under thirty minutes, bench pressing 225 lbs. ten times, and getting your cholesterol under 175 would be specific. With the latter, you will know for certain whether you have achieved it or not.

IS IT TIME SENSITIVE?

Making 1.2 million dollars over the next few years is not time sensitive. Making 1.2 million dollars by May 1, 2025, is. Running five miles in under thirty minutes, bench pressing 225 pounds. ten times, and getting my cholesterol under 175 as soon as possible is not time sensitive. Running five miles in thirty minutes by Halloween this year, bench pressing 225 pounds. ten times by January 1st of 2024 and getting my cholesterol under 175 by March of 2024 is time sensitive. The latter are clearly stated finish lines for you to cross.

Before we put this in column two, let's run it through a few more steps to ensure it's what you want to do. We set goals because we are committed to achieving them. There is nothing worse than dedicating your time and effort to a goal, and upon achieving it realizing that it wasn't what you thought it would be, or even what you wanted. Or even worse, achieving a goal and having it affect you or the ones you love in a negative way.

Write down the answers to these questions on your brainstorming sheet.

- What would stop you from committing wholeheartedly to the achievement of this goal?
- How much time and energy will you have to put into this to achieve it?
- What skills will you have to learn?
- What knowledge will you have to acquire?
- How will the pursuit of this goal and its achievement affect those in your life? (Good and bad.)
- Ask yourself, "Does any part of me object to us pursuing and achieving this goal?"

Now, considering the answer to these questions, do you still want to achieve this goal? You may need to adjust your specifics or your timetable or change the goal altogether. Make sure the goals you put down in column two are ones you are willing to achieve.

This can be a lot. Take your time and do not rush this process. When you have a specific "what" and understand your "why," the "how" will find a way of working itself out. Now take some time to understand the "why" which is truly motivating us to accomplish these goals.

PART 2: WHY DO YOU REALLY WANT IT?

There is no wrong "why." You do not need a reason to want what you want. You don't need to explain or justify yourself to anyone. The only person you need to justify this to is yourself. Whether or not you are aware of it, every "what" has a "why." Understanding your "why" helps you understand a couple of important considerations.

- What emotional want or need do I hope this accomplishment will fill for me?
- What does the achievement of this goal do for me that is even more important?

For example, achieving 1.2 million dollars is great, but what will 1.2 million dollars do for you? Is it allowing you to feel secure? Is it going to make you happy? Is it going to give you a feeling of success? Is it going to buy you freedom from the life you are currently stuck in? These "whys" are the things that are going to motivate you. These will keep you up late at night and wake you up before your alarm clock goes off in the morning. This is the fire you must fuel.

The best way I know of to clarify your "why" is to actually be in the moment you accomplish your goal and see how you feel and what that does for you. We are going to do that next.

EXERCISE: FUTURE-SELF VISUALIZATION

If this feels like an exercise you have done before, good. That means you have been practicing. For the rest of this book, you will find yourself using this skill in many ways. Column three of your worksheet is for you to write in your "why" when you are clear on it. Before you do that, though, let us complete this exercise first. You will be writing down more details about this visualization, so have a piece of paper handy. You will use this to help you achieve your goal.

Now, see yourself in the future at the specific time you have set for your goal to be accomplished. See yourself in the third person, as if you are a neutral observer. See yourself accomplishing this goal. Now build the image.

- What do you look like?

- What are you wearing?
- Where are you?
- Who is with you?

The more detail you can bring into this, the more powerful this becomes. Now write down those details. It doesn't have to be a novel. You know; red ribbon in my hair, in good shape, wearing my favorite dress, etc. When you have a good image, allow yourself to pick yourself up out of your body, travel along your timeline, however you perceive your timeline, to that future time, and settle in as your future "you." See the scene you just imagined, but through your own eyes. Take a second to settle in. If you can, imagine looking at your phone or calendar and seeing the date. If you know in advance what day of the week it will be on, bring that context into it as well.

- Do you hear anything outside of yourself?
- Are you telling yourself anything?
- What does it feel like to be in your future body?
- Are there any sensations?
- Now become aware of any emotions you are feeling.
- How are you feeling now that you have accomplished this goal?
- What is the emotional payoff?

If you feel nothing that's ok.

- Pretend and imagine if you accomplished this goal right now, what would it feel like?
- If you could feel a feeling, what would that feeling be?

Quickly write down your answers. Again, it doesn't need to be a novel.

Now get back in there. See what you see. Hear what you hear. Feel what you feel. From this vantage point in your future, having accomplished this goal, what else are you getting out of this?

- How has this affected your life in a positive way?
- What does that feel like?
- What other opportunities has accomplishing this goal opened up for me?

Don't rush it. Allow yourself to be in this moment in your future. Lose yourself in it. When you feel you have gleaned what you can out of this, come back to the present. Write down your answers on your sheet of paper.

If there is pushback or a negative feeling or something does not feel right, then you missed something, which is ok. It means that part of you is not on board with achieving this goal. Head back to Part 1 and run through the questions again, being extra aware of any resistance, and see what you come up with.

Completing this exercise thoroughly and honestly will provide you with your emotional "why" and any other positive outcomes from accomplishing this goal. These are your "whys." This is the fuel for your fire. Write down your "whys" in column three of your worksheet. Write down the details of the visual, auditory, and kinesthetic/feeling components of this future event in column four. This will provide a bit of context for you. You will be returning here again soon and strengthening this future event.

Complete this activity with all your goals. Get to a point

that when you look at this worksheet or think about your goals, there is a genuine, sincere, and powerful emotional response. With this power, our destinies are shaped. In doing this you will develop a desire so strong that absolutely nothing will stop you. This is a fire that will manifest as an unwavering persistence and perseverance.

PART 3: HOW YOU INTEND TO GET IT
By this time, you have a clear vision of your goal. You know where you are right now. So you may be asking, "How do I get there from here?" The details of your plan will depend on how big of a goal this is and what area of your life it is in. For instance, your goal might be to run a 10k race scheduled for a month from today. This might be a lot simpler to plan for than starting your own business and being free from your day job six months from today. I recommend for this exercise that you do it on one of your larger goals, and maybe you have a clear idea of exactly how you will accomplish it. Regardless of the size or scope, subject each goal to these steps.

STEP 1: THE BRAINSTORM
You should be used to brainstorming by now. This is a great technique to create choices and options and receive inspiration. Pull out a piece of paper and draw a line down the center of it. For your most important goal, allow yourself to write down, on the left side of the paper, any potential steps you may need to take or things that might aid you in accomplishing this goal.

For the 10k race, your brainstorm could include different running schedules, weight-lifting options, supplements, reading running magazines, watching videos on running techniques, investing in a good pair of shoes and running gear, dietary concerns, etc.

For the business, your brainstorm could be a lot bigger. It could include things like researching different business models, getting your business plan together, figuring out what products or services you will provide, web presence, marketing, your current financial health, financial planning, learning how to do taxes and billing, etc.

Write down every consideration you come up with. Even if it seems silly, write it down. It may have come into your head for a reason. Remember, inspiration comes in many forms. We need to make sure we are allowing inspiration to present itself. If it is just a silly notion, then you can cross it out later. Researching what is necessary to accomplish your goal is something that you should put down on this list. Google is a wonderful thing.

STEP 2: MODELING

In Chapter 9, you modeled individuals succeeding in this area of your life. Reassociate with those individuals and subject them to a different line of inquiry. This time, imagine them accomplishing a similar goal or milestone you are looking to accomplish. See them accomplishing it in as great a level of detail as you can. What do they look like? What is their posture like? What are they saying? Then lift yourself up and set yourself down inside them and as them. Now bring into this moment everything you know about this person and everything you might know about how they accomplished your goal. Then ask yourself a few questions.

- What steps did I, (say their name), take that helped me to achieve this goal?

- What skills did I, (say their name), need to achieve this goal?
- What resources (say their name), internal (traits, states of mind, motivation strategies, etc.) and external (equipment, labor, time,) helped me achieve this goal?

Allow yourself to add everything that comes to mind on the left side of the paper. And again, doing research on exactly how this person achieved your goal is something that you should put on the list.

STEP 3: REFINE YOUR LIST
You should have before you a mass of raw material. What you will do now is refine it. Go through each of these and ask yourself if it is necessary to accomplish your goal. If it is, then write it down on the right side of the paper. When you have what you need transferred over, take a minute to make sure you're not missing anything.

STEP 4: CHUNK IT DOWN
Setting a big goal, perhaps a life-changing goal, can be scary. It is easy to get overwhelmed by the magnitude of it.

For a lot of us, this has been the reason we have never pursued our dreams. When I think about a big goal, I might feel a little unsure and uncomfortable and say something like, "Wow. That's a lot. I'm not sure I can do that. Maybe I don't want to do this. After all, life isn't really that bad right now." This happens all the time. An important thing we need to be aware of is that if we try to set a goal we don't feel good about, we will find a way to not wholeheartedly pursue it. That part of us feeling uncomfortable and unsure is our subconscious mind, and we all know how powerful this can be. We need to feel confident and certain about pursuing our goals.

That is where chunking comes in. Your goal is not one big goal you have to accomplish all at once. We need to drive that thinking from our minds. Looking at our big goal this way would be akin to eating a whole turkey in a single bite. It is not possible, so it is likely that we will not even attempt it. What you have written on the right side of your paper is a whole bunch of small, very attainable goals, or bites if you will, that when completed will equal you achieving your big goal.

Draw a line under your list on the right side of the paper. Then write your goal under that line. All the activities above the line equal achieving the goal below the line.

For instance, maybe one of your chunks for starting your own business is getting a website up and running. And maybe when you think about that, you feel a little overwhelmed. All that feeling of overwhelm is telling you is that you are still biting off more than you can chew. Chunk it down even further.

- The chunk of the big goal of creating a website is still creating a feeling of overwhelm and "I can't do this."
- Chunk it down further until you have a feeling of confidence and "I can do this."
- Research website designs website platforms. "I can do this."
- Schedule an appointment with three service providers to allow them to present their services. "I can do this."
- Decide on a platform and design. "I can do this."
- Brainstorm content. "I can do this."
- Write content. "I can do this."

The real key to this is chunking it down to manageable pieces you feel confident you can accomplish. You transform this big goal you are not sure you can accomplish into a whole bunch of little goals you know you can accomplish. Knowing you can accomplish the goal quickly evolves into knowing you will accomplish the goal. By knowing you can accomplish a goal, your subconscious mind goes from protection mode to achievement mode. Chunking your goals down based upon how they make you feel allows you to focus all that you are into their achievement.

Now it is your turn. Pull out a separate piece of paper and write down every chunk on your list. Chunk each chunk down into all the things that need to get done to complete it. Write your big goals and chunks in the appropriate boxes in the Chunking worksheet at the end of this chapter.

In this chapter, you have clearly and precisely established your what, why, and how. In the next chapter, you will be firmly establishing your "when" by assigning these different chunks a specific date they will be accomplished by. More than that, you will be learning a powerful transformational technique that will allow you to focus the power of every moment of your life into the accomplishment of your goals.

CHAPTER 10 KEY TAKEAWAYS

- For a goal to be well-formed and achievable, it must both be specific and time sensitive.
- Understanding your emotional gain behind the accomplished goal is your "why."
- Your "why" is what you will use to motivate yourself to accomplish your goal.
- We can increase our motivation and the likelihood we will accomplish our "big goal" by chunking it down into smaller, more manageable, and achievable goals.

WHAT AND WHY WORKSHEET

Area of your Life	Your "Big Goal" or What	Your true motivation or "Why"	How you experienced the accomplished goal or "VAK"

PLAN YOUR WORK

CHUNKING WORKSHEET

Big Goal:	Big Goal:
Chunks:	Chunks:
Big Goal:	**Big Goal:**
Chunks:	Chunks:
Big Goal:	**Big Goal:**
Chunks:	Chunks:
Big Goal:	**Big Goal:**
Chunks:	Chunks:
Big Goal:	**Big Goal:**
Chunks:	Chunks:

CHAPTER 11

BREATHE LIFE INTO IT

"The visions you glorify in your mind, the ideals you enthrone in your heart, this you will build your life by, and this you will become."

~JAMES ALLEN

In the previous chapter, you created an excellent, well-thought-out plan that will lead you to accomplish your goals. You clarified what you want, why you want it, and how you will get it. The only thing we did not include was assigning a completion date for each of the individual chunks you have broken your big goal down into. This is not a chapter on time management. I do not want you to schedule every hour of your day, which doesn't leave any room for inspiration to happen. You will not need to know all the answers or exactly how you will achieve your goal. The next indicated right thing will always present itself if we allow ourselves to see it. Realize that once you have mastered the skills in this book, you will no longer need to know all the answers. The answers you will receive intuitively will be far more effective and more enjoyable than anything you could have come up with. You will, depending on what you believe, develop a trust or faith in your higher self, your soul or spirit, the power of your subconscious or super conscious mind, or your God.

What we will do now is take everything you have learned about timelines and apply them to your future. In particular, the timing and plotting of your big goals and all the smaller chunks you broke those big goals down into.

STEP 1: LIST YOUR SUCCESSES AND TRUTHS
Take out a piece of paper and list some of your biggest achievements so far in your life with the approximate dates they happened. Now write down anything that you know to be absolutely true, that you can remember in great detail, and that you can imagine clearly on your timeline. Holidays and birthdays are great for this. They are memorable, time specific, and you know that they happened. Don't worry if you aren't able to plot these moments on your timeline, that doesn't matter. It helps if you can, though.

STEP 2: CODING SUCCESS AND TRUTH
What you are doing in this step is developing a recognition of the feeling of "I know this to be true. This has most certainly happened."

Now pick at least three successes and things you know to be true. The closer they are to the context of your goal the better. Imagine the first one on your timeline and ask your subconscious:

I am now speaking to my subconscious. (Pause.) How do I know this experience is true?

What you are doing with this question is setting an intention with your subconscious. You are looking for a knowing. Even if you do not come up with clear details, search for the feeling of certainty and truth within it. Now step into these moments and reassociate with them. See what you saw. Hear what you heard. Feel what you felt. Think what you thought. Re-experience these positive moments in as much detail as you can. Then dissociate yourself from this moment and see it back on your timeline. Note any changes in how you see it in time.

Write down any common submodalities you might notice. Maybe there is a feeling in a specific part of your body associated with this knowing and certainty. Maybe you are fully associated in all the moments that you know are true. Maybe when you view these on your timeline, they are all the same color or size. Look for any common submodalities and write them down.

Now look back on your last three birthdays. How do you experience those on your timeline? How do you know that you had those birthdays? What you are looking for is that knowing and certainty that it is true and it has most certainly happened. Write down any similar submodalities and become very aware of that feeling of certainty and "past tense." Become familiar with that feeling. Know that feeling.

Next, think about your next birthday. Really, anything that you know will happen that you are excited about. If it is something in the same month as your big goal being accomplished, that would be even better. Holidays work well for this. Write down any similar submodalities. Is there an expectation that this will happen? A feeling that you know it hasn't happened yet but you'd be silly to doubt that it will? A feeling that you want it to happen, you know it has not happened yet, but you are certain it will happen? There is no doubt that it will happen. Become familiar with that feeling. Know that feeling.

STEP 3: PLOT YOUR GOALS ON YOUR TIMELINE

Now bring your awareness to your future timeline. Allow yourself to feel a good sense of how you perceive it. You will do this exercise on a piece of paper, but you will eventually need to project this and have a feel for it on your actual timeline.

For this, you will need your Part 4 worksheet from the previous chapter—the one with all your goals and the different chunks needed to attain those goals. You will also need a piece of paper. You will probably want to do one for each goal. I would recommend that you just do this with your most important goal for now. Once you have this down and have created a strong memory of your future, you can add some more goals in.

Turn your piece of paper so the long side goes left to right and draw a horizontal line through its center. This line will represent the time it will take to achieve your big goal. The far left is right now. The far right is the achievement date. Now chunk this down. If it is a year, break it down into months. If it is a month, break it down into weeks. If it is weeks, break it down into days.

Do not chunk it down too small. You don't want to micromanage yourself. Again, you want to allow for a little inspirational flexibility. This is key. You want to allow for the subconscious and superconscious to get involved.

Now with each of the chunks of your big goal ask yourself this, "For me to accomplish my big goal on schedule, when would this chunk need to be accomplished?" You may not know for sure, but all you need is a general sense of a good date for this chunk to be accomplished by. Take all your major chunks and plot them on your timeline. The smaller activities can be kept on a calendar or in a notebook.

I usually work this backward and then forward. I plot the chunk on the timeline, then work backward from there, making sure I have enough time to do all the activities needed to complete the chunk. I then test-drive it forward, imagining completing all the activities, and make sure it feels good. I adjust it as needed.

This needs to be a reasonable and achievable plan, and we need to consider there is only one of us and only twenty-four hours in a day. We cannot expect miracles to happen. They may happen, but let's plan for the worst and hope for the best.

STEP 4: TEST DRIVE

Read through this exercise completely before performing it. Now it is time to take your plan for a little test drive. Imagine moving forward on your timeline until your first chunk is completed. Now see that moment as being real right now, fully associate with it, see what you see, hear what you hear, feel what you feel, bring in the context of time by looking at your phone or calendar, etc. Bring into your awareness that "feeling of knowing and certainty" that this has been accomplished. Then move forward through time again to the next chunk. Fully associate with it. Now do this at a nice even pace through all of them until you accomplish your big goal. Allow yourself to reassociate with the moment you accomplish your big goal. See what you see. Hear what you hear. Feel what you feel. Become that person in the future who has accomplished this goal.

Now look back on the journey it took to get there. Remember in what ways you grew as a person because of pursuing and achieving this goal. Allow all that growth to integrate into your being. When you feel good about this moment, lift yourself up as your future-self and allow yourself to travel back through your journey, bringing with you as much insight and growth as you can, and travel back to your present moment and allow yourself to drop back into your current self. Now ask yourself, "What did I learn by accomplishing these goals that are set out before me?" Adjust your timeline as needed.

STEP 5: PLANT THE SEED

Make sure you have set aside twenty to thirty minutes for this. You have a good plan. Now it is time to plant your seed and believe that it has grown. You have a good sense of the different "chunk checkpoints" on your timeline. Now refamiliarize yourself with that feeling of knowing and certainty and any submodalities written down for Step 2. Feel that feeling of knowing and certainty.

Now imagine all your checkpoints and the accomplished goal on your actual future timeline. Allow that to settle in. Take a few deep breaths and relax. Just allow it to be. Ask your subconscious out loud to guide you in this. You are appealing to all your higher faculties. If you pray to God, bring Him into it. If this is in accordance with His will, ask Him for His blessing.

With as little effort as possible, float through your timeline and reassociate with your first checkpoint. Now imagine it in the submodalities you pulled from your successes and truths.

With as much as you can and with all you are, bring in that feeling of certainty, knowing, and truth. Imagine that you are now "remembering this moment." This moment has already happened. Allow yourself to believe not only in this moment but in your ability to create this moment.

When it feels right, continue this process with all the chunks until you have achieved your big goal.

Now do the same thing with the moment you accomplish your big goal, but add another step. Once you have made this moment as wonderful, intense, and real as possible, look back on all the chunks you accomplished and the steps you took to get here. Look at them as you looked at your previous three birthdays. See the chunks as if they have definitely happened. There is no doubt in your mind they have been.

Now see yourself through the eyes of those that are closest to you on your journey. Your spouse, children, parents, siblings, co workers, boss, or friends. See what they see. See yourself succeeding through their eyes. Describe it to yourself. Describe the changes they have seen happen in your life. What are they hearing? What are they saying and thinking? What are they feeling? Do this with as many people as you want to. There is no rush.

Now re associate yourself in that moment your goal is accomplished and focus on your breath as if you are actually in that moment breathing. Know that you are in the future moment and that future moment is now. Clear your mind of all thoughts and just focus your attention on your breath. Allow yourself to be there now.

When you are ready, turn and look back on your timeline and allow yourself to travel back through your timeline, bringing with you all the growth and knowledge you can, and allow yourself to be in this present moment now. You are almost done.

Now turn your attention one more time to your big goal. See it as done. See it like it has already happened and time just needs to catch up with it. See it now as you see your next birthday or the next major holiday you are excited about. Remember this feeling.

From now on, when you think about your big goal, think of it in this context. Excited. Certain. Patient. From now on, when you think about all the chunks and steps needed to get there, see them as already being accomplished. Again, time just needs time to catch up with them. They are already done.

The last step is to look at your future timeline and add the qualities from your past timeline indicative of positive moments. Colors, size, movement, sounds. Anything you can think of, add them to your future timeline. You know this has worked when you feel it has worked. If making it bigger or brighter or adding a different color or maybe a sound to it feels good, then do it. When you imagine any changes like this just pay attention to how it makes you feel. If it makes you feel good, confident, certain, or any number of many positive emotions, then it is probably a good thing to do. Get excited about your future, the life you have always wanted to live. Believe it will happen, expect it to happen, and it surely will happen.

I know this sounds like a lot, but it should only take about thirty minutes. Sometimes less. Sometimes more. Although it should be completed within the framework given, there is no right or wrong way to do it. This is your journey.

Please know that just to the extent that you have an open mind with this and are thorough and patient with the process and yourself, you will be astonished and amazed by the results.

And it will feel really good, like a daydream that you know will one day become reality. Please dream. Please give yourself this gift. Allow yourself to feel the power you have within you to create your own reality. Allow yourself to feel the power you have within you to believe and use that power of belief to shape yourself and your life.

I would like to share a metaphor that will help you understand what you just did in "planting the seed." When you plant a seed, you do so with the expectation that it will grow. You take all the measures you can to give it all the resources it needs to grow. You plant the seed in nice fertile soil. And once you plant it, you do the things you can to help it along the way. You water it. Make sure it gets enough sun. You may even sing to it. You love it.

The only thing you cannot do though, is make it grow. Only Mother Nature can do that. All you can do is nurture it and believe that it will one day grow. There are things, though, that you can do to prevent it from growing. The obvious: Don't water it, don't give it sun, don't do the things within your control to help it. But the worst thing you can do is doubt that it will grow. We become nervous because the seed hasn't sprouted yet. We doubt that it is ok or if we planted it ok. We wonder if we watered it too much or too little or gave it too much or too little sunlight. We say things like, "I just don't have a green thumb. I've never had any success with plants." And then we dig it up to see what we did wrong and see how it is coming along, stunting its growth and/or harming it or killing it. Then we discover that it would have sprouted soon, but by digging it up, we prevented that from happening.

What you have done in this chapter is plant a seed in fertile soil. You have planted this seed with great care and love. You have laid out before you the sun and the water in the form of your smaller goals and timeframe for them. You have shown your willingness to do what you can to get the job done. In visualizing the seed being grown, you have loved it with all your heart and all that you are. You have done everything you can at this point to help it grow healthy and strong, and you will continue to do so.

What I caution you against is "digging up your seed." This will happen when you doubt whether it will happen. This will happen when you second-guess your plan. This will happen when you doubt yourself. If doubt creeps in, as it sometimes will, just love on it and let it go. Look at your path to your goal. See how you have accomplished all the steps that make up that path. And see your goal as already being accomplished. Then turn your attention to whatever step you are working on. Focus your attention on the next indicated right thing. Just do not dig up your seed. Do not give up on your seed. You have created it. You have breathed life into it. Now have faith in yourself and your life and allow it to grow.

You have learned so much in this chapter. You can strengthen these skills for the rest of your life. I do not believe there will ever be a limit on how far you can take this process. Remember. Life gives us what we are, not what we want. If we want more, we need to become more. Practicing these exercises and applying these exercises is how you become more.

In the next chapter we will look at things that might prevent you from pursuing your goal, and we will look at motivational strategies that will help you keep your fire for change burning hot.

CHAPTER 11 KEY TAKEAWAYS

- The feeling of knowing and certainty is one of the most important feelings you can develop.

- You have events in your life that have happened and haven't happened yet but you know will happen. Within these events is the recipe for knowing and certainty.

- You do not need to know all the answers. Know that your goal will be accomplished. Be willing to do what you can to help. The next indicated right thing will be revealed if you allow yourself to be aware of it.

- Don't doubt yourself. Do not dig up your seed. Believe that it will be and know that you have within you all the power you will ever need to do your part.

CHAPTER 12

THE QUALITY OF YOUR JOURNEY

*"The most important thing is to enjoy your life –
to be happy – it's all that matters."*

~AUDREY HEPBURN

A journey of a thousand miles begins with a single step. We have all heard this expression before, and we have covered it as well in this book. We know that without taking that first step, there is no journey at all. This chapter is about helping you take that first step or helping you begin again if your progress has stalled. A thousand miles can be a long journey, so we will consider strategies to not only help you persist and persevere, but also to enjoy your journey every step of the way. In this chapter you will learn to:

Overcome procrastination.
Master motivation.
Enjoy your journey and feel successful and fulfilled now.

PART 1: OVERCOME PROCRASTINATION

Procrastination shows up in many ways. We will look at two key causes of procrastination. Waiting for things to be perfect and the fear of failure. These two things will prevent you from pursuing your goals and dreams and put them on the back burner indefinitely. Let us consider these now.

THERE IS NO PERFECT PLAN NOR WILL THERE EVER BE A PERFECT PLAN

You have created a solid plan that will lead you to the achievements of your goals and realize the "why" associated with those goals. Your plan, though, is more than likely not a perfect plan. At this point, you might have a good picture of the path you will need to take, but you may have holes in your plan you do not have the answers for. What you need to understand, accept, and embrace is that there is no such thing as a perfect plan. There never has been. There never will be.

Ask anyone who has achieved anything of merit, and they will tell you that the plan they had before they pursued their goal does not match the steps they actually took to achieve that goal. It may have been close, but along the way they faced some unexpected obstacles that made them adjust their thinking, methods, and approach. Many will tell you that inside that unexpected obstacle they found a key element to their success. On the other side of that obstacle, they found the answers and growth they needed. You must understand this, accept it, and if the moment comes, embrace it and run with it.

Remember, our exterior environment reflects our inner environment. I believe that sometimes life throws us a little test to see if we are the caliber of person necessary to live the life we are trying to live. A test of character if you will. If an obstacle arises and attempts to throw you off course, get excited about it. Even if you do not know how to overcome it, be genuinely excited that it is happening. It means you are on the path. It means you are close. Life will not give you an obstacle you cannot overcome. Life will often throw an obstacle at you just to see how committed you are to achieve your goal. On the other side of these obstacles, you will find the person you want to become and the life you want to live.

OVERCOMING THE FEAR OF *"FAILURE"*

Fear of "failure" can result from a great many things. Low self-confidence. Fear of rejection. Low self-esteem. Traumatic events as a child or adult. Maybe we "failed" at one thing and the results were painful, and because of that "failure," we do not want to try something else, even if it's totally different and unrelated. There is nothing wrong with being afraid. It is natural and not a bad thing. It means we are about to do something different, and we should be as prepared as we can be. It is just fear doing its job.

The first thing to do is examine what "failure" means to you. You have probably noticed that I have been putting the word "failure" in quotation marks. I have been doing that because at some point in our lives, someone has lied to us and told us that "failure" is a bad thing. I will say that again as you allow that to sink in. At some point in our life, someone has lied to us and told us that "failure" is a bad thing. They told us that failure brings with it negative consequences and that failure is usually a final and permanent thing. Now, whoever we picked this up from meant no harm by it. See, at some point in their life someone lied to them as well. And the people that lied to them were lied to. "Failure" is like fear; it is something we make up to protect ourselves from imagined future pain and suffering.

A presupposition of NLP is "There is no such thing as failure, only feedback." By discovering "how not to do something," we learn valuable lessons that will help us in accomplishing our objective. "Failure" is not a bad thing. Most successful people will tell you that on their path to success they received quite a bit of "feedback" on how to succeed. Our feelings and beliefs about what "failure" means are of the greatest importance. Remember, only you can assign meaning to any event or circumstance in your life.

- "Failure" does not need to create negative consequences.
- "Failure" does not need to bring us pain and suffering and loss.
- "Failure" is not final or permanent.
- "Failure" is only final or permanent if we choose to see it as such. If we choose to not accept it as feedback, choose not to learn a lesson from it, and choose to never try again, then yes, "failure" is final and permanent. The only time we truly "fail" is when we give up and quit.
- Do not quit. Do not give up. Do whatever it takes for as long as it takes and you will never be denied. Demand prosperity from life and be willing to do whatever your part is in it, and life will always give it to you.

The second thing to ask yourself is, "Have any of my failures ever killed me?" and "If I fail at accomplishing this goal, is there the potential for me to die?" I know this might seem absurd but ask yourself these questions anyway. If you feel these questions are absurd, then allow yourself to laugh, thinking about asking yourself these questions while you are asking yourself these questions.

"I mean, how silly is that? Of course, I'm not going to die if I get turned down for that promotion," or "Of course I'm not going to die if my speech doesn't go well," or "Of course I'm not going to die if my business isn't a success." Laugh out loud. Let it sink in. This is not meant to take the fear away, although it might; it is just meant to loosen you up a little bit.

The third thing to do is play the reel forward. We will often fear a potential imagined future event we have not thought through all the way. Ask yourself,

- If I do not achieve this goal, what is the worst thing that would happen?
- What is the likelihood it will happen?
- If it did happen, (again, we know it will not kill you), would it do any permanent damage?
- Would there be options available that would allow me to recover?
- Could I live with these options?"

And not just the negatives; play the reel forward on the positives as well.

- Has someone ever achieved this goal before?
- Are they human like me?
- What will happen when I do succeed?

- If at first I don't succeed, is it possible that I can find an alternative way of achieving my goal?
- What will my life be like when I accomplish this goal?
- Even if I fail on my first attempt, is it possible that I might grow from that experience and learn some valuable lessons?

As you have heard me say a few times, fear is false evidence appearing real. It is not real; we just imagined it to be so. When you subject your fears to logical questions based on actual reality and born from actual experience, you shine the light of your consciousness on them, and they begin to dissipate. Like a dark room cannot endure the flipping of the light switch, fear cannot endure the truth. You will see that all your fears are not real. Again, these questions may or may not get you past this fear, but it will certainly loosen its grip on you.

EXERCISE: FALSE EVIDENCE THAT WAS NOT REAL

In this exercise, you will make yourself aware of all the times that the false evidence presented to you by the fear of failure turned out to be not real. We have often heard, "Do what you fear most and you will conquer fear." The problem is that we have all conquered fear on many occasions, we have just forgotten them or haven't been willing to give ourselves credit for them.

Step 1: Look back at all your accomplishments in your life. Whether graduating high school or getting a college degree, landing that new job, getting that promotion, moving out on your own, giving a speech, being a parent, being a good friend, standing up for someone who cannot stand up for themselves, etc.

Step 2: Take out a piece of paper and draw a line down the center of it. On the left side, list all your accomplishments. Again, this could be anything positive you have accomplished or achieved. And there are probably more accomplishments and examples of being courageous than you are giving yourself credit for. Trust me, they are there. Sometimes just living out a single day can take more courage and bravery than we realize. We sell ourselves short when we see a situation and say, "I didn't have any other choice. That wasn't courage or bravery. I just had to do it." You have and always will have a choice. You never have to do anything. You chose to walk through fear and do whatever needed to be done. That is courage. That is bravery. Always give yourself credit where credit is due.

Step 3: Remember back to these accomplishments and answer these questions for each one. For this accomplishment:

- Was I at any time nervous about it?
- Did I have any anxiety about it?
- Did it at any point cause me to be sad or depressed?
- Did I at any point doubt whether it would turn out ok?
- Did I at any point doubt my ability to achieve it?
- Did I at any point consider giving up?
- Did I feel any negative emotions that made me want to give up?

The fear of failure can manifest in many forms. Answer these questions honestly. If you felt any of these and succeeded in any way, then you conquered your fear. Period. Write down your answers on the right side of your piece of paper.

Step 4: For the ones you answered yes to, bring yourself back to those moments of fear. Reassociate with the nervousness, doubt, second-guessing, or sadness. Just a basic emotional recognition is required for this. And when you feel associated with the negative feeling, fast forward through time and remember your moment of accomplishment. Feel proud of yourself that you did not give in to your fear. Do this with them all. It is important that you connect the fear with the fact that it wasn't real.

We will often take that one "failure" and the pain from it and with a broad generic stroke, apply it to all situations to one degree or another. This can affect our self-esteem and self-confidence in all sorts of not-so-good ways.

The goal of this exercise is for you to know that your one "failure" is far outweighed by your many successes. It is easy to grasp this concept and understand this could be true. You can understand something though, and still not know that it is true. When you allow yourself to relive your success that disproves your fear, and then you write it down on paper, you are actually experiencing it, and a true knowing only comes through experience. Understanding is a product of thinking. Our fears are below our thinking. It is there that we must deal with them. Allow yourself to experience and celebrate all your successes. Know that your fears are not real, and you do not need to allow them to run your life.

PART 2: MOTIVATION STRATEGIES

Now that you have started your journey, let's look at some ways you can keep yourself motivated and see your journey through to its completion. Whenever I talk about motivation strategies, I like to reference "the carrot or the stick." You can get the horse moving, either by positive motivation (carrot) or negative motivation (stick), or both.

Let me preface this with the fact there is no good or bad motivation strategy. One is not necessarily better than the other; it just depends on the person and the situation.

Let us consider negative or "away from" motivation. This can be anything where your "why" is a negative emotion or an aversion to something happening. This can be powerful and effective, but by motivating ourselves this way we are almost always focused on the problem. Yes, we focus on the future, but with a steady eye fixed on the rearview mirror.

Remember, we strengthen that which we give our attention to. Our subconscious mind cannot tell the difference. It just sees our heightened emotional intention and brings more of that into our awareness. Even if we achieve our goal, this taints the journey and makes it less enjoyable and more stressful than it needed to be. Now, stress is not necessarily a bad thing, especially if our motivation is to get away from a tiger, but if we don't need the stress to accomplish our goal, then why experience it?

When you designed your goals, you considered this, but that doesn't mean that along the way you will not shift your focus from "towards" to "away from." A lot of things can happen on the way to accomplishing your goals. It can be pretty easy to get into a bad mood and get discouraged. We are human. It will take what it takes. The key is to be able to recognize it when it happens and shift back to the positive.

For example, maybe your goal is to run a marathon, and you told all your friends and family about it. They may ask you how your training is going and whether you are on track in your training or not; you may feel some pressure and realize that you don't want to tell all these people you gave up or couldn't finish the race. Your original "why" was to be in the best shape of your life and feel that sense of accomplishment that comes with that. You wanted to build your confidence and your self-esteem through being disciplined. And now your "why" is tilting toward social insecurity, fear, and vanity. Again, this is not good or bad. Both can probably get you there, though one journey will probably be more enjoyable than the other.

You will have goals where you do not care if you are happy or not; you just need to get it done. I get that. When faced with emergencies, we need to do what we need to do. And you may have seen good results with negative motivation in the past. Past success can be a difficult thing to overcome. That is one of those "good is the enemy of great" type situations.

It's not about the destination; it's about the quality of the journey. It's about who you become because of taking the journey. Your life is always right now. The quality of your life is always defined by this current moment. You can be focused on negative things and be stressed out if you want to. That is your prerogative. I am here to tell you, though, that you will pay the price for that at some future date. It may not be in a similar context to your goal, but it will happen. We cannot focus on negative things and not attract more negative things into our lives. "You will know the tree by its fruit." I cannot plant a lemon tree and expect it not to grow lemons.

We all tend to motivate ourselves in a certain way. Discovering what your go-to motivation strategy is can go a long way toward increasing the quality of your life. I will share with you strategies that, negative or positive, are typically very ineffective strategies.

Fear-based motivation

Fear, not being real, is not a good thing to motivate oneself with. For example, imagining that if you do not lose thirty pounds, you will never get another date and will spend the rest of your life alone. When you realize that the fear is not true, your motivation would then go away, leaving room for compromising and bargaining with yourself.

Biting off more than one can chew

In the above example, you are focused on the end result of losing 30 lbs, instead of the smaller steps you will take that will get you there or chunking it down. We have discussed the resistance you will get from your subconscious mind with this type of strategy.

Focusing on doing a task as opposed to focusing on the task being completed

The first is potentially discouraging, thinking about all the work you must do and all the sacrifices you may have to make, while the latter is almost always positive. If we focus on all the work we must do to accomplish something, we may decide it's not worth it and decide not to do it.

When we set a goal to discipline or punish ourselves, we are doomed to fail on so many levels

I had a problem with this at one time. I gained thirty pounds during COVID. There were many reasons for this, medical and emotional, but I found that my discipline pertaining to my diet had fallen off. I was hard on myself and fought myself on this. When I had gained about ten pounds, I decided I needed to do something about this and chose to be super strict with my diet. I was fed up with my lack of discipline. This wasn't just about ten pounds to me. Invariably, when I fell short of the perfect standard I had set for myself, I reprimanded myself, and redoubled my efforts. As this ten-pound gain progressed into a gain of thirty pounds, the swings became much more acute. I was disciplining myself, and punishing myself and I didn't know it. And all it did was make the situation worse.

When I finally recognized what I was doing, I applied the

principles and techniques in this book to it. I shifted from an ineffective negative strategy to a healthier and more positive strategy of wanting to be healthy, feel good and happy, and have more energy. I lost all thirty pounds, and I genuinely enjoyed the process.

These are just a few strategies that are often ineffective. To summarize: fear-based strategies, biting off more than you can chew or not chunking, focusing on the tasks instead of focusing on the desired results, and punishing or disciplining strategies are ineffective.

CELEBRATE YOUR SUCCESS

Another way to add to the quality of your journey is to develop the habit of celebrating your successes every day. When we allow ourselves to feel good about something, we are activating the reward centers in our brain. These reward centers love to feel good about things. When they find a source that makes them feel good, they do whatever they can to put us in a position to get more of whatever that is. Let that be your daily successes. In Chapter 7, you created your Ideal Self worksheet and your Daily Success Program. These will be key in creating a life filled with consistent growth, happiness, and contentment.

Your Ideal Self worksheet was meant to show you where you are at now and where you are going, but more importantly, how far you have come. I have my Ideal Self worksheet out every time I do my Daily Success Program in the morning and in the evening. Every time I do something that aligns with my ideal self, I allow myself to celebrate that success and allow myself to feel good about that. Every time I am true to my daily intentions, in any way, I allow myself to celebrate that success. Every time I am made aware of what I wanted to be aware of for that day, I celebrate that success. You do not need to throw a party every time you exhibit a wanted trait, but at least give yourself credit for it. Allow yourself to feel good about it, even if just for a moment.

It's ok if you do something not in alignment with your ideals, exhibit unwanted traits, or get unwanted results or "feedback." Remember that there is always a lesson to be learned in these moments, wisdom to be gained, and guidance and inspiration that will allow you to become the person you need to become so you can live the life you want to live. There is no success without these moments. Allow yourself to celebrate the lessons learned, and the wisdom gained, and the guidance and inspiration that life has blessed you with. Celebrate all of it.

Celebrate the accomplishment of all the chunks of your big goals. Maybe take a little more time with this to reflect on what you have done. **Celebrate the fact that you created this moment. Remember how you saw this moment as being true and then it became true. This is critical feedback**. Allow yourself to feel the power you have to create wonderful things in your life. See how much you have grown so far. See how you have overcome any obstacles in your way. See that you learned whatever you needed to learn to accomplish this goal. See how much closer your big goal is now that you have accomplished this smaller goal. Allow yourself to feel good about your success. Allow yourself to feel happy about your growth. Allow yourself to feel fulfilled. Know that you have taken actions today bringing you closer and closer to your ideal self and your ideal life. Allow yourself to feel good about your progress.

Celebrating your successes is not some delusional practice where you are making up things to feel good about. Celebrating your successes is all about giving credit where credit is due. Celebrating your success is all about increasing the quality of your life in as many moments as you possibly can, increasing the joy and happiness you can squeeze out of every step you take. It is all about increasing the quality of your journey, being happy, joyous, and free now. Your life is right now. Celebrate it.

CHAPTER 12 KEY TAKEAWAYS

- There are no perfect plans, nor will there ever be a perfect time.
- You have overcome the fear of failure many times in your life. It has been false evidence appearing real.
- There are no good or bad motivation strategies. It just depends on what works best for you.
- Our motivation strategies impact the quality of our lives.
- Success is a measure of the quality of the journey and the person we become along the way.
- Celebrate all your successes and all your growth. We can always find things that can be celebrated, things we can feel good about, things that will all increase the quality of our lives, if we will look for them.

CHAPTER 13

YOU SHALL KNOW YOUR TRUTH

"It's not what you look at that matters, it's what you see."

~HENRY DAVID THOREAU

There have been many activities I have called game changers. Activities where I said, "If you only do one activity, do this one." The fact is that they are all game changers, but only if you take the time to do them honestly and to the best of your ability. When I originally wrote this book, these next two chapters were in Part 1. I wanted to make sure that you were ready for them before presenting them to you. That, and limiting beliefs are some of the biggest obstacles you will encounter on your journey in life.

The activities in this chapter will help provide you with a map of all your beliefs and how they are affecting your life. This chapter will not be a deep philosophical conversation. This chapter will help you uncover what your beliefs or personal truths about life are. Once you know what you believe, then you can look at your beliefs and decide if they are helping you or hindering you.

Before beginning, please take a few minutes to review the worksheets at the end of this chapter. You will be using these as you move through this chapter.

BELIEFS, TRUTH, AND CONFIRMATION BIAS (OUR SUBJECTIVE INTERPRETATION OF THE TRUTH)

Let's take a moment to define what a belief is and how you will be using it in this chapter. According to Merriam-Webster, belief is defined as,

- a state or habit of mind in which trust, or confidence is placed in some person or thing.
- something that is accepted, considered true, or held as an opinion: something believed.
- conviction of truth of some statement or the reality of some being or phenomenon especially based on examination of evidence.

Definition 1 is pretty simple. As a state of mind, a belief controls how we perceive a situation. For example, if I believe that I am not secure in a relationship, I will act in a different way than if I believed I am secure in a relationship. As a habit, a belief is set to automatically become a state of mind given a certain set of circumstances. For instance, your beliefs about yourself in a relationship might differ from your beliefs about yourself athletically. With the change of situation or context, your belief program will automatically change and run in the background.

Definitions 2 and 3 get a little more complicated, as they involve the word truth. And again, we will not be going into a deep philosophical debate on truth here. One definition in the Merriam-Webster dictionary is "a judgment, proposition, or idea that is true or accepted to be true." So, a judgment, proposition, or idea kind of leaves it wide open for interpretation. And true, or accepted to be true, makes it even more ambiguous. I get from this that truth is subjective, and as such is whatever I believe is true for me.

Our personal truths are what shape and control our subjective experience of reality and how we respond to that reality. It is through the lens of these truths that we define ourselves and our lives. Depending on the results they are producing in your life, you may consider them either wanted or unwanted, and that's if you even know that you have them. The tricky part is, if we are not aware of our personal truths, we cannot match them up to the results they are creating in our lives. All that you have is the fruit, but not the tree it fell from. When you discover your personal truths, you put yourself in a position where you can intentionally and deliberately change them and align them with who you want to become and the life you want to live.

Our personal truths affect the way we perceive our reality. Gaining understanding and awareness of this is one of the most important things you can do to increase the quality of your life. One of the main ways it affects our perception of reality is through "Confirmation Bias." Confirmation bias is a human tendency to look for and seek information that supports what we believe to be true and supports our model of reality, ignoring or filtering out information that might challenge what we believe to be true and our model of reality. It is also the tendency to interpret information in a certain way so that it supports our personal truths and model of reality. So basically, confirmation bias is our way of feeling ok and secure in the "fact" that what we believe to be true, and the way we view the world, is correct. We hear what we programmed ourselves to hear. See what we have programmed ourselves to see. Feel what we have programmed ourselves to feel. Confirmation bias makes objectivity and change difficult. It is strongly associated with, and often a manifestation of, the fear of change. We are constantly seeking balance and predictability at the deepest levels of our subconscious mind. We are constantly seeking comfort and safety and security, regardless of evidence and facts to the contrary.

Our personal truths and the confirmation bias that comes with them are not all necessarily bad. We have beliefs and personal truths that have added to the quality of our existence. One thing to consider, though, is the statement, "The enemy of great is good." A good life can become a prison if we cling to it and stop changing and growing. Confirmation bias may prevent us from finding a better understanding or a knowing that would enhance the quality of ourselves and our lives. We are limiting our growth when we close our minds and don't look at things objectively. Good or bad, wanted or unwanted, with confirmation bias, we are in a state of self-deception to one degree or another. In this chapter, you will become aware of how confirmation bias has affected your life.

IDENTIFYING YOUR PERSONAL TRUTHS
The first thing we need to do is discover what we have believed

to be true in the past and what we currently believe to be true. Once we know what these are, we gain the power to enhance them, change them, or replace them moving forward. For the rest of this chapter, you will work to uncover as many of your personal truths as you can and see how the confirmation bias resulting from these truths has affected your life. This chapter is all about increasing your awareness of your truths.

POSITIVE PERSONAL BELIEFS

You will begin this journey with a list of positive beliefs that you know to be true about yourself. I have provided Personal Truths worksheets at the end of this chapter. Most of these will start with "I am" (followed by a positive attribute), or "I can," or "I will," etc. For example, "I am good at my job," or "I can achieve anything I set my mind to," or "I will overcome any obstacles that stand between me and my goals." Change any "I am not beliefs" into the positive opposite. For example, change "I am not greedy" into "I am generous," or "I am not selfish" into "I am unselfish" or "selfless."

NEGATIVE PERSONAL BELIEFS

These will begin with "I am" (followed by a negative attribute), or "I can't," or "I am not good enough to," etc. For example, "I am bad at my job," or "I can't learn new things easily," or "I am not good enough to achieve my goal." Write your negative beliefs on your Personal Truths worksheet.

Now that we have gotten the beliefs you know you have, it is time to look for the beliefs you may not know you have, or are not very aware of. You may be wondering how you can find something if you do not know what you are looking for. We will find your hidden beliefs as scientists are able to locate a black hole. The thing that makes a black hole difficult to detect is that its gravitational pull is so strong that even light cannot escape it, making it invisible to us. They learn of a black hole's presence by becoming aware of how its gravitational pull affects the space and matter around it. They look at an area of space and say, "The only way that makes sense is if there is a black hole at the center of it." That is what you will do here.

You will look at different aspects of your life and say, "The only way that makes sense is if there is a belief at the center of it."

FEARS

The first aspect we will look at is the fears that are most common in your life. Fears result from us believing that something will threaten us or cause us pain in some way. It is a belief we will lose something we think we need or not be able to acquire something we think we need. We have discussed fears at great length, so you should have a good idea of what your more prevalent fears have been and continue to be. Write down your fears on your Personal Truths worksheet.

Now, for each fear, answer this question:

- "What must I believe to be true in order to feel this fear?"

For example, "I fear public speaking because I believe that I am not good enough and I believe that if I fail, it will negatively affect my life," or "I am afraid to leave a bad relationship because I believe that I won't be able to find anyone better," or "I believe that I do not deserve to be happy." Write down your answers next to your fears on your Personal Truths worksheet.

AREAS OF STRENGTH

What you are looking for here is areas of your life you are strong in and that you feel good about. These may be similar or the same as some of your answers in the "positive beliefs" section. This will help you identify any beliefs you may have missed. Areas of your life you might consider are self-discipline, knowledge and education, career, finances, romantic relationships, family and friends, material environment, spiritual development, health, personal well-being, personal achievements, community, or social environment. This can be any situation or set of circumstances that make you feel good when you think about how they impact your life. Maybe you are happy with the money that you make, or you are happy with how you behave in your romantic relationships, or you feel good about your physical fitness, or you feel good about people, places, and things that affect your life. Write these down on your Personal Truths worksheet.

For each area of strength, answer these questions:

- "What is it about this that I feel good about?"

    and,

- "What must I believe to be true to feel this way about this situation?"

For instance, "I feel good about my physical condition because I believe that it is necessary to feel safe, and I believe it is necessary to be considered attractive to the opposite sex." What you are looking for are the beliefs that are tied to positive situations and circumstances in your life.

AREAS OF DISCONTENT

Discontent means you are not happy with a situation or set of circumstances. What we are looking for here are areas of discontent in your life that you have not changed yet. These can be any areas of your life. Some areas you might find you are not content with could be self-discipline, knowledge and education, career, finances, romantic relationships, family and friends, material environment, spiritual development, health, personal well-being, personal achievements, community, or social environment. These are situations you might feel "stuck" in. Situations where there do not seem to be any good options available to you. Things about yourself you are not proud of or are ashamed of. Things like unwanted feelings, behaviors, or habits. Things about other people, places, or things that create a negative emotion in you. It can be anything that you do not like about yourself or your life. Write all these down on your Personal Truths worksheet.

For every one of your discontents, answer this question:

- "What must I fear or believe to be true that is preventing me from making a positive change in this situation?"

If you don't know what you believe, then start with fear.

- "If I make changes in this area of my life, what am I afraid might happen?"

And then ask yourself,

- "What must I believe to be true in order to feel this fear?" Just like you did in the fear section.

For instance, "I feel like I deserve a raise and my fear of losing my job or fear of confrontation has stopped me from doing anything about it." I might feel that fear because I do not think I deserve the raise, or I would not be able to get a higher-paying job elsewhere.

WHAT DO MY PARENTS BELIEVE TO BE TRUE?
Whether we know it or not, we have adopted beliefs from our parents. We are very impressionable when we are children, which has been a particularly good thing for the survival of our species. When we do not know how to do anything, especially when we are young, we learn from watching those around us: parents, grandparents, siblings, tribal elders, etc. We learned to mimic the beliefs and resulting behaviors and habits that enabled them to survive, become secure in the social group, and find a mate. It doesn't matter if they are positive or healthy beliefs or not. We mimic and adopt them anyway. A lot of our beliefs are layered on top of these beliefs we adopted in our formative years. Some are buried so deep it can be difficult to get to the root cause of them. And it's difficult to find something if we do not know what it is or even know that we have it. Completing the following list may provide you with some insight and direction.

Consider all the people that played a key role in your childhood; it could be parents, teachers, religious figures, older siblings, etc. It doesn't have to be an extensive list. There is room for ten people on the Personal Truths worksheet, but it may be less than that. I would just focus on the key influences. Now ask yourself these two questions about each one:

- "What character traits, beliefs, habits, or behaviors do I like about this person?"

and

- "What character traits, beliefs, habits, or behaviors do I not like about this person?"

We see things in others that we do or do not like about ourselves. Write your answers on your Personal Truths worksheet. Now for each trait, ask yourself these two questions:

- "What must someone believe to exhibit this trait?"

and,

- "Is this a trait that I also exhibit?"

If the answer is "yes," then ask yourself this question:

- "What must I believe to be true to exhibit this trait?"

Write your answers on your Personal Truths worksheet.

DREAM LIFE INCONGRUENCE

This is great to create awareness of the beliefs you have about what is and what is not possible for you and for your life. In this exercise, you will be imagining lofty dreams and goals for yourself and becoming aware of any resistance, aversions, negative self-talk, or negative imagery, otherwise known as "incongruence." When our words are communicating something like, "I am going to finish a marathon by the end of the year," but our feelings, body language, and actions are communicating something different, we are in a state of incongruence. This means at some level your conscious or subconscious mind, usually the subconscious, do not believe it can happen, or don't want it to happen.

Go back to the Two Pins in the Map worksheet on page 186. For each "Where you are going," imagine increasing the level of success you would like to achieve. Now stretch your imagination beyond what you think is possible. Imagine there is a dial that you can turn that will make your life better and better and better. Turn that dial.

As you do this, be hyper aware of any resistance you might feel. Things to look for are anxious feelings, uneasy feelings, doubt, images of failure, and any negative self-talk, posture changes, etc. If you did not come up with much resistance, turn the dial even more. What you are trying to find here is the limit of what you believe is possible for you, or if you will, your limiting beliefs. For each example of resistance, ask yourself this question:

- "What must I believe to be true for me to feel this resistance or incongruency?"

Write down and define any resistance or incongruence that you experience on your Personal Truths worksheet.

PART 3: CONFIRMATION BIAS IN ACTION

We will now look at how these beliefs may have, might have, or definitely have affected our lives. There is a column on each page of your Personal Truths worksheet reserved for just this. In completing this portion of your worksheet, you will increase your awareness of how your beliefs have shaped your subjective experience of reality. Your reality as you know it has been filtered through these belief systems. As you increase your awareness of how your beliefs have been filtering your reality, you will also increase your ability to control this and change this if need be.

It can be difficult to go back and see what you filtered out. It's not impossible, as your subconscious remembers everything, but it is difficult. Do not be discouraged if you initially come up with nothing on this portion of the exercise. If nothing pops up, imagine what you could have filtered out based upon your belief. Ask yourself these questions:

- What evidence in my life proves this belief to be true?
- How have I actively sought to support and prove this belief?
- What evidence would disprove or contradict this belief?
- How have I actively avoided evidence that may disprove this belief?
- How does this belief affect how I perceive my past?

Again, do not be discouraged if you cannot imagine anything. Just considering what you might have filtered out will communicate to your subconscious that this is important, which will increase your awareness moving forward. You will begin to see things differently in your life. Your subconscious mind will show you things that were always there that you have never noticed before. You will begin to see things in a much more objective way.

For every entry on your Personal Truths worksheet, consider how confirmation bias may have affected your life. I know this seems like a lot of work, but nothing will give you a better return on your investment of time than becoming deliberate and intentional about what you believe and examining how that affects your life. Take your time as you go through this portion of the exercise. Write down anything that comes to mind. As you go throughout your days and recognize your bias in action, add them to this worksheet. Gaining awareness of something and writing it down is powerful.

Mastery is all about increasing your awareness of yourself.

It is about increasing your ability to see your thoughts, emotions, actions, intentions, reactions, and beliefs, objectively, pausing, and consciously deciding how you want to show up in any given moment of your life.

In this chapter, you have increased your awareness of what you believe to be true and how those beliefs have affected your life. You have compiled six pages of life-changing information and insight. In Chapter 14, you will decide what you want to do with these beliefs. You will learn how to overcome limiting beliefs, strengthen empowering beliefs, and install altogether new beliefs.

CHAPTER 13 KEY TAKEAWAYS

- Our beliefs control how we perceive, think about, feel about, or respond to any given set of circumstances in life.

- Confirmation bias acts to make us aware of information that supports our beliefs and filters out information that might contradict our beliefs. This can be discovered at this present time or as we survey our past and decide what it means to us.

- We can trace all our behaviors, emotions, thoughts, and fears back to the belief that created them.

- By understanding what you believe to be true and how it has affected you so far, you can now align your beliefs, deliberately and intentionally, with your ideal self and your ideal life.

PERSONAL TRUTHS WORKSHEETS

Positive and Negative Beliefs

Positive Belief	Confirmation Bias	Negative Belief	Confirmation Bias

					Fears	
					What must I believe to be true?	**FEAR BELIEFS**
					Confirmation Bias	

STRENGTHS BELIEFS

Strengths	What must I believe to be true?	Confirmation Bias

DISCONTENTS BELIEFS

Discontent	What must I believe to be true?	Confirmation Bias

OTHER PEOPLES BELIEFS

Other people's traits you like and do not like	What must they believe to be true?	Do I exemplify this trait?	What must I believe to be true?

					Dream Life Incongruence	**DREAM LIFE-LIMITING BELIEFS**
					What limiting belief must I believe to be true?	
					Confirmation Bias	

CHAPTER 14

YOUR TRUTH SHALL SET YOU FREE

"A belief is only a thought you continue thinking; and when your beliefs match your desires, then your desires must become a reality."

~ ESTHER HICKS

In the previous chapter, you took a thorough look at what you believe to be true, and you became aware of how these beliefs have affected your life. The first time I did this exercise, I was left with a big mess. There were so many ways of looking at what I had written down. It seemed like I had created more questions than answers. In this chapter, you will work toward clarifying which beliefs you want to keep and strengthen and which ones you do not want to keep. If you're not living the life you want to live and are not the person you want to be, then your beliefs aren't in alignment with how you want to live and who you want to be. It is time we did something about that.

PART 1: YOUR TOP TEN BELIEFS
The first thing you will do is condense the six worksheets from the previous chapter and come up with a list of your top ten most important and influential beliefs. You will apply the techniques in this chapter to these ten beliefs. When you have learned how to use these techniques, you can apply them to any other beliefs you want to change.

You more than likely have a lot written down and have a good idea of your most influential beliefs. This is a good place to start. This will change and evolve as you gain more understanding and awareness of these beliefs. Now take out a blank piece of paper and, starting at the top, write your top five wanted and top five unwanted beliefs and number them one through five in the order of their importance to you. Number one would be of greatest importance to you. I chose the beliefs associated with the best parts of my life and those associated with the areas that needed the most improvement. I am sure you have some other beliefs and questions and loose ends on the six worksheets from the previous chapter you need to do something with. You may not have five wanted or five unwanted beliefs to put down. That is perfectly ok. The key with this is to be objective and honest. Do the best you can. More is always being revealed.

Now go back through your worksheets and look for similar beliefs and number them if they are directly related to your top five wanted or unwanted beliefs. For instance, my number one wanted belief was "God will make all things right when I surrender to His will." I wrote the number one next to beliefs like "I am guided and directed by God," "I am a child of God," "Everyone else is a child of God too, and thus my brothers and sisters," "I and the Father are one," and "It is the Father in me that doeth the works," etc.

My number one unwanted belief was, "I will not be ok if I am alone." I wrote the number one next to beliefs like "I am unhappy alone," "If I am abandoned then I will not be ok," "If I am rejected then I will not be ok," and "If I am abandoned or rejected, it will be forever." These are all similar, and I believe they are directly related to and stemming from the same core belief and the event that created it.

(Since writing this I have applied the technique Timeline Cleansing to this, and I've found the root moment and these related beliefs have been diminished considerably. Now they are merely echoes and rumors of something that might have been.) This should help you narrow down your list a bit and should provide more insight as to the extent that these beliefs have affected you.

Do this with all five of your wanted and unwanted beliefs. If you have beliefs left on your worksheets not directly related to your top five, then compare them to each other and see if they are directly related to each other. The key here is for them to be directly related. If you are not sure that they are directly related, then leave them alone for now.

When you have come up with your top five wanted and unwanted beliefs, write them down on the Your Truth Shall Set You Free worksheet at the end of this chapter. Highlight or underline any beliefs on your six worksheets from the previous chapter that did not make either top five, so you can easily find them later.

PART 2: POSITIVE INTENTION

Just like there is a positive intention for every wanted and unwanted behavior, there is also a positive intention for every wanted and unwanted belief. Our beliefs are there to protect our three primary instincts: social, sex, and survival. What we will be looking for is the emotional gain that the belief provides us and the instincts it protects. The belief doesn't matter as much as the results it is creating in your life and the lives of those around you. Again, the belief is just a means to an end.

For instance, my number one wanted belief, "God will make all things right when I surrender to His will," seems like a spiritual and altruistic belief, and it is. Now where I got that from, though, was the second half of the Serenity Prayer, "Knowing that He will make all things right when I surrender to His will." The positive intention was that I found comfort in this belief. It took away my fear of people and fear of economic insecurity and allowed me to walk through some difficult times in my life without freaking out or making things any worse than they already were. It has helped me accept things I cannot change. The positive intention when I accepted this belief was freedom from fear and increased emotional and mental security. The positive intention behind this now is joy and hope and love and serenity. This belief has protected all three of the instincts.

Another example of this would be my number one unwanted belief, "I will not be ok if I am alone." This has affected almost every relationship I have ever had. My fear of abandonment and my fear of rejection stemmed from this. I feared being abandoned or rejected because I believed that I would not be ok alone. This belief has manifested in so many ways. Sometimes it manifests as the fear of failure (because if I failed, you would abandon me and reject me, and I would not be ok alone), clinging, neediness, insecurity, manipulation, controlling behavior, people-pleasing, and on and on and on. All these behaviors I have exhibited in response to this belief have had the positive intention of keeping me safe and happy and secure. This belief kept me safe by driving me to always be in a relationship so I would not be abandoned and rejected and alone. I believed I would not be ok if I were alone. This belief protected all three primary instincts.

I hope these two examples show you what the positive intention of a belief can be. When we did this same exercise on your unwanted behaviors, you were looking for a positive intention so you could find more resourceful and positive ways of achieving the same positive intention. And, often, the behavior we employed was not achieving the desired outcome anyway. This is the same with beliefs. We may have a belief meant to keep us from being alone that is causing us to be alone, or a belief meant to protect us from failure that is actually causing us to fail. Once we have the positive intention we want to achieve, we can consider the belief and see if it's working for us or not. Write down your belief's positive intent, primary instincts protected, and any other insights this provided on your worksheet at the chapter's end.

For each positive intention you are using these beliefs to achieve, ask yourself these important questions:

- Do I truly want or need this positive intention? If so, why?
- Are the behaviors resulting from this belief accomplishing the desired outcome?
- Is it creating the opposite of the positive intention?
- If there were a better way, would I be open to change?

PART 3: STRENGTHENING WANTED BELIEFS

You now have a good idea of your wanted beliefs, their positive intent, the instincts they are protecting, and whether they are getting the job done. Let's look at some ways to strengthen these beliefs and look at other ways you can achieve the same positive intention or protect the instinct at the root of it.

Write down your top five wanted beliefs and their corresponding positive intentions and instincts being protected. Ask yourself these questions:

- Is this belief satisfying my want or need for this positive intention?
- Do I want more of it, a higher quality of it, or a greater degree of it in my life?

You have gone to great lengths to come up with both your ideal self and your ideal life. Will this belief get you there? Brainstorm now on all the ways you can both strengthen this belief and aid this belief in accomplishing the positive intention.

For instance, my number one wanted belief of "God will make all things right when I surrender to His will" had the positive intention of love, joy, hope, and serenity. When I first adopted this belief out of necessity, I had little joy, hope, or serenity in my life. So how could I strengthen this belief and what could I do to create more love, joy, hope, and serenity in my life?

I looked for more evidence and information that supported my belief. I strengthened my belief by going back through my life and seeing how all things in my life were all right. This was like a conscious and intentional confirmation bias session. I looked at all the evidence that proved that it was true for me. Evidence like "life hasn't thrown anything at me I couldn't handle." There was a time when my oldest son, when he was really young, was in the hospital. I prayed in the hospital chapel, telling God I would do anything if He would allow my son to be ok. There was an experience I had when I was seventeen and I thought I was dying, and I prayed to God, asking for His help. There was October 27 2013, around 8:30pm. I was lying on my bathroom floor, beaten and brutalized by my alcoholism, unable to stop drinking and on the verge of losing everything, and I surrendered and became willing to do whatever He would have me do to not live that life anymore. There was the moment I knew that my career at the time was not my path anymore, and I was afraid to step away from that security. I told God I would do whatever He would have me do, and my life has never been better. And on and on and on. You get the idea. I wrote all this down. It is not as powerful if we do not write it down. We need to think it, feel it, and see ourselves write it.

Even while continuing to reinforce this belief, I still had a lot of moments when my positive intentions of joy, love, hope, and serenity were not being satisfied. There were parts of my life that still suffered, parts of my life I had not surrendered yet. I had to find ways to support this belief and its positive intention. I had to adopt other supporting beliefs and increase my joy, love, hope, and serenity through other means. I wrote down some of these supporting beliefs on my Personal Truths worksheet from the previous chapter and mentioned them earlier in this chapter. These included beliefs like "I am a child of God. As my Father, He loves me and would never give me anything I cannot handle" and "I want to be reasonably happy and of service to others," and "I am guided and directed by God," and "Everyone else is a child of God too, making them my brothers and sisters, and I will love them with all that I am," and "I and the Father are One," and "It is the Father in me that doeth the works," and the belief that "His will for me will be more glorious and wonderful than anything I could ever imagine," and so on. These beliefs and corresponding behaviors responded to slightly different life situations, but all supported the positive intentions of joy, love, hope, and serenity.

These developed over my entire lifetime. What you can do with this exercise, though, is speed up the process a bit. Ask yourself, "What other beliefs do I have that will help me achieve the same positive intention? Not only that, what are habits that I can create that can help me achieve this positive intention?" You worked on this a bit in Chapter 6, but it is worth repeating here.

Some habits that I have adopted that help me create more joy, hope, love, and serenity in my life are doing a love list as often as possible (love), saying the Serenity Prayer daily (serenity), doing a gratitude list as often as I can (hope), and intensely being in this moment through meditation and prayer (the simple joy of being). I have set an anchor for acceptance and surrender. Most of these beliefs are a part of my ideal self, and as such, I make myself aware of them twice every day during my daily success program, like the one you created in Chapter 8.

With this practice, I am constantly intending to live up to this belief. With all these things supporting the efforts of my number one belief, my life is filled with love, and joy, and hope, and serenity.

It is my firm belief that everyone wants to be happy, that they want more joy and peace and love in their lives. That they want to feel safe and secure and be free of fear. Remember, a belief is just a means to achieve these positive intentions.

This process is simple and can be applied to any wanted belief and its positive intentions. Write down all your answers on the worksheet at the end of the chapter.

THE PROCESS
Write down the wanted belief and its positive intentions.

Find all the supporting events, evidence, and information you can for your belief.

Write down any other beliefs that share some of the same positive intentions.

Write down any habits you have or can develop that would help achieve the same positive intentions.

EXERCISE: BELIEF SUBMODALITY ELICITATION
We will now look at how you are experiencing these beliefs at a structural or submodality level. For each belief, imagine or remember yourself embodying this belief. If you are having a difficult time, tell your subconscious, "Show me how I experience this belief." It may be a memory or an imagined event.

When you have it in mind, run it through the submodality checklist:

- **Visual-** Location of image, size, is it framed like a TV or panoramic, black and white or color, moving or still, associated (seeing through your eyes) or dissociated (seeing as if a neutral observer)
- **Auditory-** Volume, Speed, Location, Tonality
- **Kinesthetic-** Location of feeling, shape, movement, pressure, color
- How do you see this belief?
- What sounds do you hear?

- What are you saying to yourself?
- What bodily sensations and emotions are you feeling?
- What is your physiology like?
- What is your posture like?
- How are you breathing?

Write these on the worksheet at the end of the chapter. After you are done with all five, look at any similarities they share. These similarities are key. What this exercise allows you to do is discover how you code positive beliefs. This awareness will allow you to access the states associated with these beliefs and use these submodalities to change and create other beliefs. You will do the same thing on your unwanted beliefs next.

PART 4: UNWANTED BELIEFS

You have identified what your unwanted beliefs are, and any supporting beliefs that came up, in Chapter 13. You have also identified your positive intention of these beliefs and the instincts they are protecting. And you expressed a willingness to change. Now it's time to take a deeper look at these beliefs and see if we can loosen them up a bit.

Remember Hebb's Law, neurons that fire together wire together. Beliefs are a large set of neurons that have been fired together and wired and strengthened. These beliefs have had their confirmation bias supporting and protecting them for a long time. We need to bring into your awareness contradictory events, evidence, and information to create a bit of doubt in the truth of this belief for you.

When trying to understand unwanted beliefs and why we have them, it helps to look at how we are communicating these beliefs to ourselves and to others. Complete the following exercise before moving forward. It is important that you complete this exercise before reading on.

Exercise: Take out a piece of paper and write down your five unwanted beliefs. For each one answer there are two questions:

- "What exactly do you believe to be true and how has it manifested in your life?"

And then,

- "What else can you tell me about this belief?"

Make it as conversational as possible. If it helps, speak your answers out loud and record them. Then transcribe them onto the piece of paper.

Okay. You can read on.

An important thing to understand is that we believe the things that come out of our mouths and the things we say to ourselves. Our subconscious trusts us and considers self-talk as programming. It takes what we say as true and important and seeks to support and strengthen it through confirmation bias.

Now I will introduce what NLP calls "meta-models." Among many other things, these influence how we communicate our reality to ourselves and to others, and how we perceive what others and the world are communicating to us. Our reality is purely subjective and is the sum total of our lifetime of experiences. They are filters, like beliefs, as they stand between the truth and our subjective experience of the truth. There are a whole bunch of meta-models, and I will not overwhelm you with them all. In these exercises, we will just be focused on some of the meta-models and how they pertain to language. By learning about these meta-models, I became aware that I had been creating and strengthening my limiting beliefs with my self-talk and with how I was communicating these beliefs with others. The funny thing about limiting beliefs is that they are not real. They are created by us or accepted by us. They are only there because we continue to accept and strengthen them. Our verbal communication is a huge part of this.

GENERALIZATION, DELETION, AND VAGUE LANGUAGE
Generalization is a process in which we take one set of learning and apply it to other situations with similar variables or contexts. Generalization can be very useful. A good example of this would be learning to tie your shoes. Once you learn how to do it, you don't have to relearn every time you tie another set of shoelaces or a different type of shoe or that kind of knot on something else. Learning to ride a bike is another good example. You don't have to relearn to ride every different bike.

Generalization can also be counterproductive and limiting. That is why it is so important to become aware of what you are generalizing in your life. Examples of potentially negative generalizations might be asking a girl out and getting rejected and then you say things like, "Girls never want to date me." Or, burning your hand on the stove and saying things like, "I don't want to cook. I always end up hurting myself." Or you try to learn how to ski and it doesn't go well, and when invited to learn how to scuba dive, you say, "Oh, that seems complicated. I'm not really that good at learning new things." Whether we say these words out loud or internally to ourselves, this type of generalization can be very limiting.

VAGUE LANGUAGE OR DELETION

Deletion happens when a key piece of information is missing in a statement. Consider the following statement. "Bad things are always happening to me."

- What specific bad things?
- How are they bad?
- How do they happen to you?
- Do they only happen to you?

Consider the following statement. "I am getting really frustrated about how I react poorly in situations like that."

- How am I frustrated?
- How did I react?
- What situations?

What we need to become aware of is our vague language. When we say and hear vague language, we leave a lot to be interpreted by our subconscious mind. When we do not get down to specifics, our subconscious mind can generalize this and apply this perspective to all types of situations. Remember, we trust ourselves and take the things that come out of our mouth literally. We believe what we say is true.

EXERCISE: GET REALLY SPECIFIC

Step 1: Take out the piece of paper that you wrote on earlier with your answers to the two questions, "What exactly do you believe and how has it manifested in your life?" and, "What else can you tell me about this belief?"

Step 2: Look for any generalizations that may be present in your statements. Things you want to look for are phrases like "I always," or, "they never, all of them, every time they…" Key in on the words "always," "never," "all," and "every." These are Universal Quantifiers. Ask yourself these questions about each of your belief statements. Open your mind and allow yourself to be objective:

- Is this, or has this belief always been true for me?
- Has there ever been an instance in which this belief was not true for me?
- What evidence is there that could challenge the truth of this belief for me?
- Is this or has this belief always been true for everyone else?
- Has there ever been an instance in which this belief was not true for someone else?
- If the opposite of this belief were true, how would that change my life?

Step 3: Other words to become aware of are words of possibility and necessity. Words like, "can" or "can't," "could" or "couldn't," "must" or "have to" or "need to," and "should" or "shouldn't."

Challenge "can't" and "couldn't" statements with the following questions. For all these questions, keep an open mind and allow yourself to consider the possibilities:

- What would happen if I could do it?
- Has anyone ever done this before?
- Is this humanly possible to do?

Challenge "must," or "have to," or "need to," with the following questions:

- What would happen if I didn't do it?
- Who says that I have to, must, or need to do this thing? (Is it me or someone else?)
- Are there any alternative options?

Challenge "should" or "shouldn't" with the following questions:

- I should or shouldn't according to whom? (Is it me or someone else?)
- What would happen if I decided not to do it?
- What would happen if I did it?

Step 4: Other words to look for are unspecified pronouns. There are well over 100 pronouns. Some examples are words like they, them, theirs, us, we, those, everyone, everything, nothing, nobody, etc. The key with any of these is to get specific with exactly who or what you are referring to. By listing your answers to these questions, you see how your language is not matching up with reality.

Challenge these pronouns with these questions:

- Who specifically are you referring to? List them.
- Is it really everyone or everything?
- Who or what specifically are you referring to? List them.
- Who or what are examples to the contrary? List them.

Step 5: Ask yourself the following question for each one of your beliefs.

- Could this belief be based upon inaccurate information or a misinterpretation of reality?
- Should I adjust the way I describe and communicate this belief to myself and to others?
- What would be a more accurate and more realistic description of this belief?

Step 6: Now, answer these two questions. "What exactly do you believe to be true and how has it manifested in your life?" and "What else can you tell me about this belief?" Make it as conversational as possible. If it helps, speak your answers out loud and record them. Then transcribe them onto the piece of paper. Has anything changed? If so, update your belief on your worksheet at the end of the chapter.

The exercise you have just completed was meant to loosen up your beliefs. All it takes to overcome a limiting belief is a small change in perspective. This small change in perspective, over time, creates a different belief. Having done this exercise, you will more than likely catch yourself using these generalizations and deletions and vague language. If you add this to your daily awareness intention during your morning program, you will increase its positive effect on your life. During the day, as you catch yourself using these language patterns, quickly say the change or correction out loud. Remember, you said the inaccurate language out loud, and your subconscious heard it, so you need to offset this by speaking the more accurate language out loud as well. You can also include this instance in your evening program under "successes." This will also give you more time to contemplate exactly how this vague language may have affected your life, and encourage you to be more aware in the future of your language.

EVIDENCE TO THE CONTRARY

By running your beliefs through the questions above, you have no doubt come up with some evidence that your belief may not be 100% accurate. Write any events, evidence, or information you uncovered that contradicts your limiting beliefs on your worksheet at the end of the chapter.

Look for things like instances that this was not true for you, or it was true and you overcame it. Remember, fear is not bad, especially if we find the courage to walk through it. When you find these moments where you proved your belief wrong, allow yourself to associate with the experience and view it in as much detail as you can. See what you saw. Hear what you heard. Feel what you felt. Think what you thought. Show your subconscious that your belief is not 100% accurate. Write these moments down on your worksheet. It doesn't have to be a novel. Write just enough for you to remember it.

Now look for instances where this was not true for other people.

- Someone has accomplished what you believe you cannot accomplish.
- Someone feels a way you do not believe you can feel.
- Someone acts in a way you do not believe you can act.
- Someone out there is living the life you believe that you cannot live.

Find those examples and write them down. It can be anyone from celebrities to family members to religious leaders to the janitor down at your local YWCA. It doesn't matter how they did it. It doesn't matter what their childhood was like, what their family was like, where they grew up, or how the politics of the time affected them. Your mind will try to go there. It will say things like, "Yeah. He did it, but…" Everything after the "but" is a limiting belief. Do not allow yourself to get that far. If someone out there is doing what you believe is impossible for you to do, then write it down. Let your subconscious mind hear you say their name in your mind, feel yourself writing the name down on paper, and see this evidence on the piece of paper. Let your subconscious see it is possible, and that its belief to the contrary is not 100% accurate.

PERHAPS THERE IS A BETTER WAY
Overcoming a limiting belief is like overcoming an unwanted behavior, just at a deeper level. When we wanted to overcome our limiting behavior, we had to uncover the positive intention, replace the behavioral response to the situation, and make sure that we still satisfied the positive intention. This last part was important because the positive intention is why we were using the behavior or belief. If we do not address the "why," we will just deal with symptoms, which can manifest as another unwanted behavior or belief. You can choose to deliberately and intentionally satisfy your "why." That is what you will do now.

Like you did with your wanted beliefs, you will look for other beliefs that you have that satisfy the same positive intentions. For instance, the positive intention for my number one unwanted belief, "I will not be ok if I am alone," was to feel safe, secure, and happy. This belief protected my primary sex and social instincts, which both influence my survival instinct. What we are looking for in this exercise is any wanted beliefs or contradictory beliefs we have with the same positive intention and any habits we have or can create that also support our positive intention and protect our instincts.

A belief that helped me overcome my unwanted belief was my number one wanted belief of "God will make all things right when I surrender to His will." It protects all my instincts, makes me feel safe and secure, and allows me to set aside things that would normally make me unhappy. When I think about not being ok alone, I remind myself of this belief, that no matter what happens I will be ok. Other beliefs that support my positive intentions are, "I am a child of God. As my Father, He loves me and would never give me anything I cannot handle," and "His will for me will be more glorious and wonderful than anything I could ever imagine," and "The level of my serenity is directly proportional to my acceptance of the fact that I cannot control people, places, or things."

I looked at why I was alone and why I thought I would be alone. I looked at my fear of rejection and did more work on that. What I realized is that the only reason I would be alone would be that I decided to be alone. I realized that no matter how alone I felt, there was always someone I could help and provide service to. There are always opportunities to serve our fellow brothers and sisters. And a funny thing happens when I do. I make friends and feel a part of something, as opposed to feeling alone. And being a good human being and a good friend makes me feel so good and so happy. This also satisfied my need to feel safe and secure. I realized that when I am alone, the things within my control are the same as when I am not alone. Nothing changes.

I also did a brainstorm on things that make me happy that I can do alone. The list was long and included things like writing, reading, watching TV, working out, meditating or praying, taking a walk in nature and hanging out with some furry woodland creatures, playing video games, doing a love list, doing a gratitude list, listening to music, and listening to an audiobook, just to name a few.

Remember, people always make the best choice available to them. What you are doing with this exercise is giving yourself options to choose from. You are giving yourself other means of accomplishing the desired outcome, or "why." When we satisfy our "why" in healthier and wanted ways, we decrease our need to use unwanted behaviors and beliefs to satisfy the "why." We are teaching ourselves a better way to live. Include a lot of these new beliefs and habits in your daily success program. Intend to do these things and consciously satisfy your "why"s, rather than reacting to them with the same old belief program.

Sometimes these big beliefs, with lots of positive intentions, can take a little time to unravel. And rightfully so. We want and need a lot of these positive intentions to survive. We have to make sure we are not rash or hasty with this. Patience is a virtue when dealing with beliefs. It took a while to turn my belief of "I will not be ok alone" into "Everything is exactly as it is supposed to be, exactly at this moment" and "I know that everything will be ok if I continue to do the next indicated right thing."

EXERCISE: BELIEF SUBMODALITY ELICITATION

We will now look at how you are experiencing your unwanted beliefs at a submodality level. Just like you did for your wanted beliefs, imagine yourself embodying each belief in your life.

If you have a difficult time, tell your subconscious, "Show me how I experience this belief." It may be a memory or an imagined event. It may just be a general sense. Do the best you can with this.

When you have the experience in mind, run it through the submodality checklist:

- **Visual-** Location of image, size, is it framed like a TV or panoramic, black and white or color, moving or still, associated (seeing through your eyes) or dissociated (seeing as if a neutral observer)
- **Auditory-** Volume, Speed, Location, Tonality
- **Kinesthetic-** Location of feeling, shape, movement, pressure, color
- How do you see this belief?
- What sounds do you hear?
- What are you saying to yourself?
- What bodily sensations and emotions are you feeling?
- What is your physiology like?
- What is your posture like?
- How are you breathing?

Write these on the worksheet at the end of the chapter. After you are done with all five, look at any similarities they share. These similarities are key. What this exercise allows you to do is find out how you code unwanted beliefs. With your awareness of these submodalities comes your ability to change these submodalities. When you change the structure of any memory or imagined event, you change the meaning of it. This includes beliefs. Write down all your answers on your worksheet at the end of this chapter.

PART 5: THE SUBMODALITIES OF CHANGE
In this book, you have learned the importance of the structure of our experience as defined by submodalities, and you have done quite a bit of work with these building blocks of reality. What you will do now is use the submodalities of your beliefs to weaken and or remove your unwanted beliefs and install a new, wanted belief.

EXERCISE: SUBMODALITY MAP ACROSS
Step 1: Choose a top five unwanted belief you would like to remove or weaken. You have written down the submodalities of this belief, but experience it again to re-familiarize yourself with it. Look for the content of this memory. For instance, "I am in the hallway at work getting ready for a presentation. I see the closed door to the meeting room. I see my boss inside wearing a nice suit." You do not need to write this down, just get a few more details on it. Now break state.

Step 2: Think of an old belief that you once had that you now know is not true. Something like "I'm afraid to get in the pool because I'll drown," or "Santa Claus is real," or "I can control how other people think and feel about me." Whatever it is, choose one you know is no longer true, and preferably one you can imagine in great detail. Now write down all the submodalities of this belief.

- **Visual-** Location of image, size, is it framed like a TV or panoramic, black and white or color, moving or still, associated (seeing through your eyes) or dissociated (seeing as if a neutral observer)

- **Auditory-** Volume, Speed, Location, Tonality
- **Kinesthetic-** Location of feeling, shape, movement, pressure, color

Step 3: Now it is time to map the content of the unwanted belief into the structure of the belief you know is no longer true. This is best to do with a partner, but simply record it and listen to it if you don't have one.

UNWANTED BELIEF

Let's say that in the above example of waiting to give a presentation at work, your submodalities would be that you are associated (seeing through your own eyes), the image is life-size and black and white, there is no movement, there is no noticeable sound, you feel tense through your entire chest, your heart is beating in your chest, and your breathing is shallow. Your content of this experience includes waiting outside in a hall to give a presentation, the door is closed, and you see your boss through the window wearing a nice suit.

OLD UNTRUE BELIEF

Let's say that when I think about not being afraid to swim anymore, I see myself standing next to a pool (dissociated). I see an image about the size of a computer monitor, it is over to my left side, it is in color, there is movement, the sound of people swimming is coming from the center of my head and is relatively quiet. My posture is very erect, there is tingling going up my back, my breathing is steady, and other than that, there is no feeling.

What you will do now is see the content of your unwanted belief in the submodalities of the old untrue belief.

See the image of you waiting in the hall, but see this scene as if you are seeing it on a computer monitor, see yourself on this screen waiting in the hall. Now put it off to your left side, now see it in color, now imagine that there is movement. If there is any discernible sound, hear it in the center of your head and make it relatively quiet. Now make your posture erect, imagine a tingling going up your back and make your breathing steady.

Write this down and either have someone read it to you or record it and play it back to yourself. When you read your version of this, allow time between each instruction to allow the change to be made. Stay in this state as long as it feels right to do so. Then break state.

Once you have broken state, think about that unwanted belief again. How certain are you now that this belief is true for you? At the very least, it should feel a bit different. Sometimes it takes time to rewire. If it still feels strong, then go through this process again. You can even try another old untrue belief. The key with this is to experience your unwanted belief the same way that you experience an old untrue belief, to experience the unwanted belief as "That is no longer true for me."

Having the proper expectations of this process is critical. Anytime we are doing change work like this, we are dealing with complex interconnected belief systems and all the memories and emotions and thoughts associated with them. These systems have been fired and wired many times. Now, some of these memories and emotions and thoughts that are a part of this belief are also connected to other beliefs and emotions and thoughts. And those beliefs are connected to other beliefs, and on and on and on. It can take time for the system to settle and find a new balance. Be patient, though. Look for and recognize the change that will surely come.

I used this technique on one of my worst fears, the fear

of abandonment or my belief of "I will not be ok if I am alone." In my mind, the image I had was me as a boy, lying on a bed with wrinkled blue sheets, with my hand grasping the sheet. The submodalities were bigger than life, associated (seeing it through my eyes), in color, moving. There is the sound of me not being able to catch my breath and get a full cry out, just a quiet and distant sound of me crying, that tight knot in the chest, and the feeling of the bed underneath me.

My old untrue belief was me being afraid to speak in the meeting room at my old job. The belief could be defined as "I am going to start sweating and not be able to finish my presentation." I see this now as associated (through my own eyes); I see a hallway and an open door, life-size, still, and in black and white. There is no sound. There is a consistent, easy feeling throughout my body, and it has a nice light, vibrational quality to it. There is tension from shoulder to shoulder, about twice as intense as my total body feeling. I feel relieved.

I mapped this across by seeing the wrinkled sheet life size, in black and white, and still. No sound. And I imagined the light tension in my body, the heightened tension between my collarbones, and the feeling of being relieved.

Amazing things can happen when you do this exercise. When I broke state and then went back to this moment, it was different. I saw it as dissociated, standing up, looking out my bedroom door out into the hallway. All the other qualities were the same. I saw the hall in the home as I saw the meeting room from the hall at my old job. My fear of abandonment rapidly diminished, as did my belief of not being ok alone.

It didn't stop there, though. My subconscious took me on a little adventure. Suddenly, there was movement in my memory, and I walked out of my room, and there was a person present. I heard myself tell them I love them and I'm sorry because I believe I used to take this moment out on them. Then I saw two more people present and realized that they were a positive result of this situation happening. There was color, and the feeling of love and peace. I threw this little bit in because sometimes your subconscious wants to take you for a ride. I recommend you allow it to, just so long as it feels right. When you knock down a domino, sometimes that domino finds another and another etc.

In this chapter, you have learned, and hopefully experienced, quite a few ways to change your beliefs. If you do just one of them, you will see noticeable results in your life. If you systematically practice and employ all these techniques, the results will be staggering. Again, reading about change, and deciding to change, does not bring about change. Only action brings about change. The more you put into this, the more you will get out of it.

CHAPTER 14 KEY TAKEAWAYS

- Beliefs, like behaviors, have a positive intention or a "why."
- By finding other ways to satisfy the desired "why," we can strengthen our beliefs or weaken them, depending on the case.
- How you communicate to yourself and others, your language, has the power to create and strengthen beliefs. It has the power to change and remove beliefs as well.
- If your beliefs aren't supporting you in becoming the person you want to become and living the life you want to live, then change them.
- As you have heard so many times in this book, you have the power to change your mind. This is something completely within your control.

YOUR TRUTH SHALL SET YOU FREE WORKSHEET

					Top 5 Unwanted Beliefs
					Positive Intention and Instincts Protected
					Is your positive intention being achieved?
					Events, evidence, and information contradicting your belief
					Perhaps there is a better way
					Sub-modalities of your wanted beliefs

YOUR TRUTH SHALL SET YOU FREE WORKSHEET

Top 5 Wanted Beliefs	Positive Intention and Instincts Protected	Do you want this positive intent? Is it being accomplished? Are you open to a better way?	Supporting Beliefs, evidence and habits	Sub-modalities of your unwanted beliefs

CHAPTER 15

YOUR OMEGA STATE

"I am here for the purpose and that purpose is to grow into a mountain, not to shrink to a grain of sand. Henceforth will I apply ALL my efforts to become the highest mountain of all, and I will strain my potential until it cries for mercy..."

~OG MANDINO

You have done so much work on yourself. You have seen growth and change happen in your life. You and your life are changing before your eyes. And there is this feeling developing within you. You may not know exactly how to describe it or even know that it is there yet. When we get right with our past and begin to master ourselves, our whole life changes for the better. Even if it was already good, it gets better and better and better. This is the path you are on. It is a journey that will last a lifetime. Your future holds many moments, obstacles, and successes that hold the seeds of growth and wisdom within them.

You will continue to evolve. To change. The person you were a year ago will be a much different person than the person you are going to be a year from now. More is always being revealed.

I would like to share a story with you that holds many parallels to what you are learning and what you will learn in the next two chapters.

It is a lovely fall day and the whole town is excited about this year's wood chopping competition. The reigning champion has had little competition in the past few years, but this year it looks like he has met his match. The whole town is abuzz with talk about how this new, stronger challenger, who is younger by thirty years, will take the title from the seasoned champion. The champion has been the champion for so many years now. How long could he possibly keep this up?

He wasn't always the champion, though. There was a time when he didn't even know how to handle an ax, let alone chop through logs at a championship level. It took all the moments of his life to shape him into the champion he is today. The tales the champion could tell you about his life are filled with experience and wisdom. Obstacles faced and overcome, adversities faced and overcome, challenges of all kinds faced and overcome. Every time he has persevered and overcome one of these tests, he has gained the strength and wisdom that can only be gained through experience.

Now, the challenger is no slouch. He is young and strong, with a fiery determination to conquer the world with a single stroke of his ax. The challenger reminds the champion of himself when he was that age, so young and filled with so much potential. The world can be anything he wants it to be. The challenger is eager to claim the title and prove to himself and the world that he is the best ax man there has ever been. He is in the best shape of his life. He is stronger than he has ever been. He is well-fed and well-rested and ready to go.

As the competition is set to begin, the challenger is all fired up and filled with an intensity like he has never known. He looks over his right shoulder, where he sees the champion putting his wood-chopping gloves on. The champion looks to be in great shape for the match. He has been doing some training as well and seems very calm and peaceful. Maybe a little too calm and peaceful, he thinks. The challenger, though, sizing up the champion, sees that he is much bigger and stronger than the champion. He is quite confident, yet not overconfident, that his day has indeed come. He knows he will have to deliver the best performance of his life to beat the champion.

A moment of silence stills the scene, seemingly even the birds can't make a sound. Champion and challenger. They are back-to-back, axes in hand, three logs in front of each of them awaiting their imminent destruction. It's the deep breath before the plunge. The silence is abruptly broken by a gunshot starting the competition and the furious sound of wood being chopped by these two giants of the sport.

About midway through their first log, both contestants seem in fine form. The champion has a nice smooth rhythm going on, yet the challenger hears that the champion's strokes are not falling as hard, or as frequently as his own. This gets him even more excited, and makes him even more sure of his victory, adding even more fuel to the fire. The challenger begins chopping faster and harder.

The challenger finishes his first log and jumps over to the next. He becomes aware of the fact there is no noise coming from the champion. He isn't chopping any wood. The challenger thinks to himself, "I got him. The old man doesn't have it in him anymore." Then, a couple of moments later, he hears the champion chopping again. "Not sure taking a break was a good idea. Not sure what he was thinking," said the challenger as he lets out a confident chuckle.

The challenger finishes his second log and excitedly jumps over to his third and final log, when he becomes aware again that the champion is taking another break. "I hope he is ok and hasn't hurt himself," the challenger says to himself. Then he hears the champion start to chop again. "Well, I guess the champion still has a little fight left in him. Good for him. He can have his moral victory, though. I'll take the title." Supremely confident and in fine shape, the challenger continues to lay waste to the poor third and final log. The challenger is so excited. Another five good ax strokes and he will be the new champion.

The sound of a gunshot stills the scene. The challenger looks at the ax in his hand, and looks down at his third and final log, and realizes that he still has a few strokes to go. Stunned, he turns around to view the champion, ax at his side, three logs completely chopped in half. The champion had done it again. The challenger can't believe it. Then the crowd cheers and celebrates the champion's success.

After the champion receives his trophy, the challenger, dazed and confused, approaches the champion meekly. He asks the champion, "How did you beat me? I don't understand. I am bigger and stronger and in better shape. We both used the same regulation axes, and the logs were all the same size. And I can't be sure about it, but I think you took a couple of breaks as well. My ax strokes were harder and faster. I just don't understand. How did you do it? How did you best me?"

To which the champion responds, "I have been chopping

logs since before you were born. I have chopped logs in every situation you can imagine. In a blizzard, in a thunderstorm, in the searing summer heat. I have chopped logs waist-deep in a river during a flood. I have chopped logs on a mountainside during a forest fire. I have chopped logs with all manner of injuries. Heck, I've even chopped logs with a broken ax. And not only have I defended my title too many times to count, but before I was champion, I lost more wood chopping competitions than I would like to count. I bested you because I was the more experienced ax man."

The challenger lets that sink in. He says to himself, "Yes, it sounds like the champion has a lot of experience and wisdom, and in those days was much bigger and stronger, but how did he best me this time? I chopped harder and faster, and my technique was flawless, and I didn't take any breaks. How did he do it?" Turning to the champion again, he says, "I'll give you that. You definitely have more experience than me, but I'm still confused. I chopped harder and faster than you, and my technique was flawless, and I didn't take any breaks. How is it that you still beat me?"

The champion, with a bit of hesitation in his voice, says to the challenger, "I'm not sure I should tell you. You see, the reason I bested you was due to the wisdom that I gained from all the logs I have chopped, and in all the situations that I have chopped them in. With that wisdom came growth and joy and peace. It made me who I am today. I'm not sure I want to share the wisdom with you because I don't want to deprive you of that growth and joy and peace. You see, it's not about the obstacle being overcome or the goal being achieved, it's about the person we become while we are overcoming that obstacle and achieving our goal."

As the champion turns and walks away, the challenger

pleads with him one more time to tell him how he did it. The champion turns and with a sigh, says, "Ok. I will tell you. You had mentioned that you heard me taking a couple of breaks. This was not true. I was not taking breaks. When you heard my chopping stop, it was merely because I was busy sharpening my ax. That is how I beat you. I had the sharper ax."

There can be many parallels drawn from this story. Many morals to the story, if you will. It will mean something different to everyone. Every time you read it or a version of it, it will mean something different to you. That is because the person reading it will be different. You will be a different person.

In this story, the stronger and bigger challenger is bested by the more experienced champion. You can take this to mean, "Work smarter, not harder" or "There is always a better way of doing things" or "The ax is me, and the log is my life; by sharpening myself, I increase my ability to handle life." There are so many ways of looking at this, and they are all correct. I look at this story in all these ways too. Whatever meaning this has to you is the exact meaning it was meant to convey.

For the rest of this chapter, try to see this story from a different angle. The challenger and the champion are the same person—one a younger version of the other. The champion, having lived all the moments of his life since he was the age of the challenger, has learned many lessons. He has gained wisdom through experience. Like the steel ax head, he was forged and made stronger by all the moments of his life.

At both moments of his life, he showed many virtues. As his younger self, he worked hard at his craft and put a lot of energy into becoming the most magnificent physical expression of himself. He also believed in himself and believed he could do anything he put his mind to. He was confident but not cocky. He was a beautiful human being. As his older self, he is still healthy and strong. He has a wisdom and a strength of character that only comes through experience. He is peaceful and calm. He is humble. He, too, is a beautiful human being. There is nothing wrong with either of them. Both are exactly as they are supposed to be, exactly at that moment.

"Wisdom and strength of character that only come through experience." There are two ways we can learn the lessons we need to learn that will help us grow into the person we are meant to become. We can have the growth happen to us, or we can actively seek it out and accelerate the process. Either way, good or bad, the growth occurs. When we allow growth to happen to us, growth default mode, if you will, it can come in many forms. Now, we all know from experience that sometimes we learn a lesson the hard way. And many people would say there could have been no other way for this to happen. And they would not be wrong in saying this. Whether we believe it to be true or not, we are right.

I would like to present a different perspective on this. I believe, and I have experienced, that if I seek the growth out, I do not need to learn it the hard way. I believe we learn the hard way because we have missed opportunities to learn it the easy way. The hard way is life's way of pushing the issue. It doesn't matter why we missed the opportunities to learn the lesson the easy way. Maybe we weren't ready. Maybe we weren't looking for it. Whatever the reason, what happened cannot be changed. It's over. What we can do, though, is seek out the lessons and wisdom and increase our awareness of them in our lives moving forward. We can grow intentionally rather than by default. You don't need to suffer or toil or experience adversity to grow as a person, or to grow spiritually.

Now back to the story. The younger, stronger version was bested by the older, wiser version.

- What would it have been like if the younger version had stopped and sharpened his ax as well?
- What if he had learned some of the lessons his older self had learned?
- What if he had overcome some of the obstacles that his older self had overcome?
- What if he had persevered through some of the adversities that his old self had?
- What if he had experienced some of the moments that his older self had experienced?

"Wisdom and strength of character that can only come through experience."

We have spoken quite a bit about the fact that our subconscious mind cannot distinguish between imagined or real, especially when the experience is intense. Consider all our fears, for instance. If there is not a bear or tiger involved, then the fear is purely imagined, though we act as if it is true. We have all experienced this to be true. Every one of us. You have seen, though, that we can use our subconscious's lack of discrimination to our advantage by doing and practicing the techniques and exercises in this book. We can use this to influence and program our subconscious minds. We can use this to imagine moments and glean some of the experience and growth in character we would have gained had we actually lived them. Nothing is as effective as the real thing. This is true, but the stronger your imagination becomes, the easier it will be to influence and program your subconscious mind.

The champion told his younger self,

"I have been chopping logs since before you were born. I have chopped logs in every situation you can imagine. In a blizzard, in a thunderstorm, in the searing summer heat. I have chopped logs waist deep in a river during a flood. I have chopped logs on a mountainside during a forest fire. I have chopped logs with all manner of injuries. Heck, I've even chopped logs with a broken ax. Not only have I defended my title too many times to count, but before I was champion, I lost more wood chopping competitions than I would like to count. I bested you because I was the more experienced woodchopper."

- What if the champion got more specific about each of these experiences?
- What if the champion shared with the challenger all things these experiences taught him?
- What would happen if our future-self could share with us the lessons we have learned in all the experiences between now and then?

The champion could have elaborated a bit more.

"I have been chopping logs since before you were born. Thirty years of chopping wood has given me a great level of confidence and belief in myself. When I was your age, I had a lot of belief in myself, but some level of doubt or insecurity always weakened it. I have learned through experience to wholeheartedly believe in my chopping abilities." The lessons he learned were to be confident, believe in himself, and be fearless.

"I have chopped logs in every situation you can imagine. In a blizzard, in a thunderstorm, in the searing summer heat. I have chopped logs waist deep in a river during a flood. I have chopped logs on a mountainside during a forest fire. I have chopped logs with all manner of injuries. Heck, I've even chopped logs with a broken ax. I have learned that no matter the situation, there are definite keys to success. I had to be in good physical shape. That was key. I had to be patient and pace myself to last long enough to get the job done. There was always that knot or oddity about the wood that I learned to anticipate and overcome." So, the lessons would have been that there are success principles that are true in any situation. Stay healthy, learn to be patient, and learn perseverance and determination; you never know how or when you might need it.

"And not only have I defended my title too many times to count, but before I was champion, I lost more log chopping competitions than I would like to count. I have challenged and been challenged by so many men. It's only when I stopped measuring myself against these other men, and began to measure myself against my greatest potential, that I finally became the champion I am today. I wasn't competing with you today. All I was doing was striving to be the best person I could possibly be at that moment. I was striving to be better than I was yesterday and, take another step toward my ideal." The lesson here is that growth always happens within you first. The exterior world is only a mirror reflecting back to us who we truly are. If you want your life to improve, then start with the man in the mirror.

There are a lot of pearls of wisdom to be had here: Keep our bodies healthy, learn patience, develop perseverance and determination, build confidence and a belief in ourselves by overcoming fear, and all the power we need is within us; we must only develop and strengthen it. A lot of these life lessons are pretty common and basic. We do not need adversity to learn these and develop these, although adversity is always available to us if we need it.

THE OMEGA STATE AND OMEGA ANCHOR

How does one go about learning these lessons and gaining this wisdom intentionally? One obvious way is to seek the information and model the people that have exemplified the wisdom you seek. Look at their lives, how they got to where you want to go, and what traits they exemplied to get there, listen to them, read their books, etc. Or, do it by strengthening a trait or belief you already have, as you did in the previous chapters. You have done this a couple of times already. You will take a slightly different approach this time. What you will be developing is your Omega State and creating your Omega Anchor.

The anchors you have learned to create are a method of creating a conditioned response you can use in certain situations in your life. This conditioned response is a state of being; a blend of beliefs, emotions, thoughts, physiology, etc. You learned that you can fire your anchor when you want to, which brings you into this state and all its resources.

You may be wondering why I named this the Omega State and Omega Anchor. Omega is the last letter of the Greek alphabet. We hear "alpha" a lot. Alpha is the first letter of the Greek alphabet. I chose Omega because you need to go through all the other letters before you get to it. Just like how you can't get to your future-self without going through all the other versions of yourself first. With this state and anchor, you will be skipping the rest of the letters of your alphabet. We condition an anchor to allow us to respond to a trigger with a programmed state. The ultimate trigger, or Omega Trigger if you will, is your life, to which you are the programmed response.

What you will be doing with your Omega State and Anchor is preparing yourself to respond to the rest of your life.

When I started doing anchors, I had anchors all over my

body. I had a piece of paper with all the anchors and all the VAK associated with them. I recommend you do this as well, but simplify it as much as you can. I condensed mine down to eight and kept them on a three-by-five card. I had an anchor on each finger that I would fire with my thumb for confidence, discipline, serenity, energy, courage, speaking, writing, emotional security, and shining light. I changed these a bunch of times.

Today I only use one anchor, my Omega Anchor, which I alluded to earlier in the book. That doesn't mean I won't create anchors for specialized situations. If the situation arises where a new conditioned response will help, then I will create one. I will walk you through how to create your omega state and omega anchor now.

FUTURE-SELF MEDITATION

We haven't spoken a lot about meditation, nor will we. There are so many great books out there on the subject already. The future-self meditation is a meditation in that it requires focused concentration and witnessing. Instead of focusing on your breath and witnessing your thoughts in the present moment, you will focus on actually being yourself in the future and witnessing your thoughts and meditating from that perspective.

I originally began doing this meditation as a tool for conscious creation. I needed a context for this meditation, an environment I could create in great detail and come back to and continue to add detail and depth to. This leverages the belief that we become what we think about most, and Hebb's law, that neurons that fire together wire together. Every time I do this meditation, I tell my subconscious self, "This is what I want, make me aware of everything in my life that will help me get there." Every time I do this meditation, my internal resistance and limiting beliefs (fear of failure, economic insecurity, low self-esteem, self-doubt) weaken and my future-self and future life begin pulling me toward it. This works to consciously create your future and allows you to access your future internal resources now.

CREATE YOUR FUTURE ENVIRONMENT
My future-self begins his meditation by waking up in his king-sized bed in his mountain retreat. He looks to the right and sees the sun rising over the mountains. He gets up and walks out his bedroom door, feeling the movement of his body through space and the feel of his feet on the carpet and the pressure of gravity pulling him down. He walks down his staircase, feeling the wood banister in his hand. He pauses at the mid landing, looks to his right and sees his family sitting on the couches next to the river stone fireplace. His mother and his son and daughter on one couch. His father and his father's wife on the opposite couch. He hears them say good morning. He looks to his left and sees his library and back door. His two oldest brothers are sitting in lounge chairs at the opening of the back door. His other brother is out in the beautiful green meadow with his family. He continues down the stairs and into the foyer. To his right is his den. To his left is his dining room, kitchen, hall to the family room and door to the three-car garage. He turns left, walks through the living room and to his library. He sees the books he has written and his podcast and video equipment. He turns right and walks outside; he hears his two oldest brothers saying his name and experiences his other brother and his family coming up and giving him a big hug. He then turns back into the living room and sits in his wingback chair at the head of the couches. In front of him is his family, a beau-

tiful wooden coffee table, and the river stone fireplace and its wonderfully warm and comforting fire.

Notice the details. As I did this, I noticed more things like the type of chairs, the brand of kitchen equipment, the width of the floor planks, the warmth of the heating elements under them, the feel of the shag carpet in the living room, the warmth of the fire on my skin, the feeling of my brother's hair as I kissed his forehead. The environment became more detailed and richer every time I did this. It doesn't have to be this detailed the first time you do this. The first time I did this it was just a general sense of dimensions and clips of household stuff from memories.

Now it's your turn. Imagine yourself ten years from now, or even five years from now. Whatever it is, make it a moment in which you know you have accomplished your big goal. It will be like, "I can't believe it all came true." It can be any environment. It can be an office boardroom, or a sunny beach, or the top of a mountain. The more details you can bring into it, the better. Visualizing the environment in great detail and walking through it puts you in a light state of self-hypnosis, which gives you better access to your subconscious mind. And there should be a place within this imagined environment in which you can sit down and meditate.

THE MEDITATION

Before you begin, choose a place to set an anchor. To begin, still in this future environment, I settle into my wingback chair, acknowledge my family, tell them I love them, and they walk outside. I look into the fireplace, feel the warmth of it on my skin, take a few deep breaths, feeling my back against the chair, my arms on the armrests, my feet on the ground. Focusing on my breath and the warmth of the fire on my skin, I close my eyes in the future, I empty my mind, and everything else falls away. With each breath in, I think, "breathing in." With each breath out, I think, "breathing out." When I get caught up in thought, I bring myself back to this. "Breathing in," then "breathing out." This is all about focusing and concentrating my awareness on the breath. This type of meditation quiets my conscious mind. This makes room for my higher faculties. I do this for five minutes or until I feel like I have sufficiently stilled my mind.

Once I have stilled my mind, with my eyes still closed, still associated with myself in the future, I feel the outline of my body and where it touches the chair and the floor. I feel the warmth of the fire, etc. I then become aware of the quality of my character.

- What do I believe to be true now?
- How am I wiser for having taken this journey?
- What have I learned along the way?
- What obstacles have I had to overcome and how has that allowed me to grow?
- I imagine my ideal self and all the qualities and traits he embodies. I see what I see. I hear what I hear. I feel what I feel.
- I then imagine what I must be thinking in this moment.
- I imagine what I might be emotionally feeling in this moment.
- I imagine what my posture and my breathing are like.
- I imagine what I might believe to be true in this moment.

- I imagine the feeling of accomplishment, gratitude, and joy.
- I make that moment as wonderful as possible and when it is at its peak, I set the Omega Anchor.

You can ask your future-self any questions you want. Maybe losing weight is your biggest goal. You might ask things like, "What does my physical being feel like? How healthy am I? What was it like to lose all the weight? How did I lose all the weight? How did I keep it off all this time? How do I feel now that I am my ideal weight? Other than losing weight, how has this journey changed me and allowed me to grow? They can be vague or specific. See what you would see. Hear what you would hear. Physically feel what and how you would feel. Imagine how good it feels to be lighter and healthier in every way. Then imagine what you would be thinking in this moment. Imagine what emotions you might be experiencing at this moment. Imagine what your posture and your breathing are like. Imagine what you might believe to be true in this moment. Imagine how good you feel about yourself and how losing weight has impacted your life. Make that moment as wonderful as possible, and when it is at its peak, set your Omega Anchor. This is the beginning of your Omega State. You will continue to enhance this state and continue to tie it to the anchor you just set. Just like you did earlier, you will begin to stack anchors. Now break state.

When you are ready, fire your anchor. Be your future-self. Like any anchor, this will take time to strengthen, but you should see immediate results with this. You can tailor this experience to whatever your big goal is. The key is that you actually do this, and do it to the best of your ability, with hope and positive expectation in your heart.

STRENGTHEN YOUR OMEGA STATE
Write down any insights or information you may have received during your first stint as your future-self. Ask yourself these questions:

- What obstacles did I see that I overcame?
- What would I have had to learn to overcome that obstacle?
- What did I notice about my future-self's character and beliefs?
- What traits did my future-self embody?
- What else of note did I learn through this meditation?

Answer these questions as thoroughly as you can. Particularly focus on the lessons you had to learn and how that affected your character and beliefs.

I will share with you an example from my life. In December of 2020, I was doing a future-self meditation and while fully associated as my future-self, I saw a long fast that I have always wanted as being completed. So, the fast would be the obstacle. When I asked my future-self what I had to learn to fast this long, I was surprised at the answer I received. My answer was, "We don't have to do this fast to become the person we want to become. We can merely decide to become that person now." Before this moment, I had a belief of "The person I will become during this fast will be the one that God uses as an instrument of His peace." I felt like the rest of my life was on the other side of that fast. That until I fasted, I could not do what I needed to do. I felt I was not good enough as I was.

This was one of those moments where the surface explanation doesn't even begin to describe what was going on within me. Within days, I began experiencing my timeline in a strange way. Any time I walked down a sidewalk or a hall, anything long and straight, I felt as if I was on my timeline. It felt like a home stretch. Like my future was assured and I could sprint down and claim it. It felt foreign and unsettling. I tried to explain it to others, but I'm not sure they understood. I felt like maybe I didn't have to wait so long or try so hard to get the results in life I sought. I knew that something was about to happen. This subsided after a while, but the confidence and certainty, the faith it imparted lasted and grew. This all came as a result of an epiphany I had while having a conversation with my future-self.

Then one day in late April 2021, I experienced that timeline again. I felt like I was overcomplicating something. Shortly thereafter, I was inspired to write the first edition of this book. The thing I learned and the growth I received through the future-self meditation in December 2020, was a certainty and level of belief that I had never known.

This will feel a little like timeline work, like you did in Chapter 5, and it is. It can be as thorough as those exercises if you like but does not need to be. Look at your timeline between now and that future moment you experienced. Ask yourself:

- What obstacles will I need to overcome to get from here to there?
- What lessons will I need to learn to get there?
- How will I have to change and grow as a person to get there?

Write these answers down. You do not need to save them. I just want you to see yourself writing them down. What you are looking for in this exercise is what the challenger wanted from the champion in the ax-sharpening story. You are looking for opportunities for growth and wisdom in your future.

Now that you have done this part of the exercise, it is time to do your future-self meditation again. Begin it just the way you did before. Take time to experience your environment in as much detail as possible. Take a tour. Walk around. Experience this environment with all your senses. What are you seeing? What are you hearing? What are you feeling? Every time you do this, try to bring in a little more detail than the time before and try to make it more realistic than it was the time before. It is important that you do not rush this part.

Find a nice spot in this environment to meditate. Focus on your breathing as you did before, until your mind is quiet and still. See what you would see. Hear what you would hear. Feel the physical sensations you would feel. Match the posture and breathing. Find the emotions involved in that future moment where you are living your dream in every way.

- Imagine how you would think in this future moment.
- Imagine how you might feel in this future moment.
- Imagine the strength of your character in this moment.
- Imagine what you would believe to be true in this moment.

Now bring to mind your ideal self and the list of all the qualities and traits it embodies. As your future-self, look back on your timeline to the present moment. Then ask yourself some questions. Mine were:

- What do I believe to be true now?
- How am I wiser for having taken this journey?
- What have I learned along the way?
- What obstacles have I had to overcome and how has that allowed me to grow?

These questions will usually be different every time you do this.

Beginning now and moving forward, you will finish this exercise in a slightly different way. In that future moment, when you have the moment at its peak, imagine that your future-self's body is superimposed over your current self's body. So, they are sharing the same space. Sharing the same moment. As much as you can in this moment as your current self and your future-self, embody your positive future-self traits. Be that future you, now. Make it as magnificent and as wonderful as you possibly can, and when you feel like this moment is at its peak, re-fire your Omega Anchor and hold it as long as this moment is at its peak. Then break state.

There is no difference between your future-self and who you are now. You are both of those people. You can obviously be that future version of yourself, because you will be that future version of yourself. Just because you haven't experienced all the moments yet between now and then, doesn't mean you can't sharpen your ax now.

This exercise serves two purposes. It programs your subconscious mind and tells it what it needs to help you create for the future. And it allows you opportunities to receive insights and inspiration. The more you do this, the clearer your destination, and the path to reach it, will become. Feelings of self-doubt, fear of failure, low self-esteem, and a number of other fears and limiting beliefs will diminish. The more often you practice being your more evolved future-self, the faster you will become your more evolved future-self. I do a future-self meditation, to one degree or another, every single day. I try to do it first thing in the morning or right before I go to bed, or both, but what really matters is that it is done consistently. Every time I do this, I try to experience it in as much detail as possible and with as much physical sensation and emotional strength as I can. I make it as magnificent as I can.

USING YOUR OMEGA ANCHOR
I use my anchor almost every day. I use it any time I am believing, fearing, thinking, feeling, or acting in a way that falls short of the ideal. I will provide examples below.

USE IT TO OVERCOME A LIMITING BELIEF
The other day I was thinking about some famous authors I wanted to meet. I felt this resistance inside of me that ended up being self-doubt. It was the feeling that "I am not as good as those authors." I fired my omega anchor, and it dissolved the self-doubt present at that moment. My posture changed, my breathing changed, and I entered into my omega state. From the perspective of that state, I realized that all these authors were imperfect human beings like I am. They put their pants on one leg at a time just like I do. I remembered that soon I will overcome that self-doubt, and remembered that in the future I will meet these authors. This did not remove the limiting belief from me; that took a little bit more work, but it increased my awareness of it and loosened it up quite a bit. When you feel like you are acting out a conditioned response based upon a

limiting belief, fire your omega anchor and see if that can give you enough relief to break the pattern.

USE IT TO OVERCOME FEAR

I shared with you in the previous chapter how changing the submodalities of a belief will change the belief itself. The example I gave you was my fear of abandonment that stemmed from a moment when I was a child. In the thirty-three years or so since that moment, I have strengthened that belief and fear by acting upon it countless times. There have been beliefs and fears I have created since then that are based upon this fear, but separate. I have taken out the main root, but there are still straggler beliefs and fears to deal with. However, whenever I experience a fear associated with the fear of abandonment, I fire my omega anchor. There is no fear in my omega state and my omega state is more powerful than this fear. If the anchored state is stronger than the unwanted state, the anchored state should win out. If it doesn't, then maybe this fear is still rooted in something much deeper and stronger. All this means is you have become aware of a fear to work on, and you will just have to do more intensive work on it as you did in the previous chapter. So, if you are feeling a little afraid or worrying about something, fire your omega anchor and try to see it from a different perspective.

USE IT TO OVERCOME A THOUGHT PATTERN

I use this to stop my mind from thinking patterns I don't want it to think. I fire my omega anchor when I'm trying to sleep and my mind won't shut off. I fire my omega anchor whenever I am thinking about something that I cannot control. This allows me to see it more objectively and usually stops that thought from becoming a negative emotion like anxiety or worry. I fire my omega anchor when I am thinking negative thoughts about myself or my life situation. It allows me to see myself and my life in a much more objective manner again, minus any insecurity, self-doubt, or fear that may be lingering in the shadows. The "me" in my omega state has control over his thoughts; not perfectly, but better than I have now. Changing the state you are viewing life from changes the life you are viewing. Remember, you become what you think about most. If you are suffering from "stinking thinking," fire your omega anchor and put a stop to it.

USE IT TO WITNESS AN EMOTION

Emotion can be tricky. By bringing our emotions and our omega state together, we are allowing ourselves to feel those emotions in the best state possible. While evaluating and feeling those emotions in the omega state, we are bringing to bear all our future-self's wisdom and experience, witnessing the emotion from an elevated level. From this point of view we are better prepared to ascertain why we are having this emotion, to decide what this emotion means to us, and to decide what we are going to do moving forward, having experienced this emotion. In no way should we refuse to feel an emotion. We can choose, though, how we want to experience this emotion.

As you move forward and continue to grow and evolve, so will your omega state continue to grow and evolve. Every time you do your future-self meditation and reset your anchor, it will grow and evolve. Every time you fire your anchor in your day-to-day life, it will grow and evolve. The key to this anchor is to strengthen it every day. Whether in the morning or at night or on your lunch break, or any other time, you will need to take ten minutes and strengthen it. Bring yourself back to your omega state and that future-self that has all the answers you seek. Be the most magnificent version of yourself for at least ten minutes per day. Make it as real and intensely wonderful as you can. And reset your anchor. You will become what you think about most. The neurons you fire together will wire together. Before you know it, you will become that future-self.

These are just a few examples of when and how your omega state might benefit you. Nothing is ever 100%, and everyone's experience is unique. The degree that your anchor helps you will depend on a lot of factors. The stronger you make the omega state activated by your anchor, the more powerful the results will become. Like you have read probably too many times in this book, repetition, repetition, repetition. Practice, practice, practice. Thinking about change and wanting to change does not bring about change. Only action brings about change.

I have taken you on quite a ride in this chapter. This is some next-level stuff. It's like the Law of Attraction and NLP had a baby, and that baby hypnotized itself so its juggernaut subconscious mind could come out and play and manifest greatness. If you have made it this far and applied the principles with all the determination and passion you have in your heart, you will have changed for the better. You will have set things in motion that will coalesce and form the life of your dreams. If you haven't applied yourself as much as you would have liked to, that's ok. Any of these techniques, practiced and applied consistently, will improve the quality of your life to the extent that you practice and apply them. You own this book. You can come back and do the rest of the work when you are ready or as needed. There is enough in this book to keep you busy growing and evolving for a very long time. Every time you read this book you will get something different, because the person reading it will be different.

You have only one chapter left. Open your mind and heart and allow yourself to see, hear, and feel whatever is in this final chapter that is meant for you. There is something that you need to read, and I am not sure what that thing is. It might be a single word or phrase that triggers a chain reaction within you. One never knows when or how inspiration will come. Inspiration will always come if we open our minds and hearts, believe that it will come, and we allow that inspiration to flow through us.

CHAPTER 15 KEY TAKEAWAYS

- You will learn many lessons and grow in a great many ways over the course of the rest of your life.

- You can use your imagination and your future-self meditation to anticipate how you will need to grow and what lessons you may need to learn, so you can begin to sharpen your ax now rather than later.

- In creating your Omega State and Omega Anchor through your future-self meditation, you have both programmed your subconscious mind to bring your awareness to opportunities to make this happen, and you have found a way to be your ideal self now.

- Practice and strengthen your Omega Anchor every day.

CHAPTER 16

YOUR LIFE IS BUT A REFLECTION OF YOURSELF

"A man only begins to be a man when he ceases to whine and revile and commences to search for the hidden justice which regulates his life. And he adapts his mind to that regulating factor, he ceases to accuse others as the cause of his condition and builds himself up in strong and noble thoughts; ceases to kick against circumstances but begins to use them as aids to his more rapid progress, and as a means of the hidden powers and possibilities within himself."

~JAMES ALLEN

"Life doesn't give us what we want, it gives us what we are. If we want our lives to change, we have to change ourselves. If we want something different, then we must be willing to be different. If we want more, we must first become more." You have no doubt made positive changes to yourself and your life. You have developed a willingness to do things differently. You have become more and will continue to become more for the rest of your life.

I have written a bit about the idea that life is our mirror. That everything we experience "out there" is merely a reflection of what we are "in here." Our physical being, financial status, career, relationships, and standing in our social circle or community are all reflections of our quality of being at any given moment. You can take this metaphorically or literally, depending on what you believe. Either way, by adopting this idea, we can use the world as a measuring device to let us know how far we have come and to show us how far we still have to go. We can use the world to reveal to ourselves the things hidden and not-so-hidden that we can improve on, which will allow us to continue to grow. See, there is always room to grow.

In this book, you have worked diligently to uncover the things within yourself that are holding you back. You have discovered these fears, beliefs, thoughts, emotions, and behaviors that were like chains holding you back from becoming the person you want to become and living the life you want to live. As long as you are chained to your past, your progress will always be hindered.

In this chapter, you will understand and become aware of the ways you can use the external circumstances of your life as a tool to increase your growth even further. You will learn to use your life as a mirror to show you the things in you that are still holding you back from becoming your best self and living your best life.

LIFE IS YOUR MIRROR – THE WORLD IS HAPPENING TO YOU
I have no doubt that you have experienced this idea working in

your life to one degree or another, and we have discussed this part in Chapter 3. We know that we have complete control over our beliefs, fears, thoughts, emotions, and actions. We know that no person, place, or thing can directly make us believe, fear, think, feel, or do anything we do not want to. We know that we have no direct control over people, places, or things. All we have control over is how we allow them to affect us and how we respond. Knowing these things to be true, it stands to reason that, "Whenever I am disturbed, for any reason whatsoever, it means there is something wrong with my thinking." Whenever we are disturbed, it is because we are choosing to be disturbed. We can respond to that given situation in any way we would like to. The question is, do you want to continue to be disturbed, or would you like to show up differently?

Here are some examples of day-to-day situations you might find your reflection in. Being stuck in traffic. Having a tough day at work. When someone is irritating or bothering you in any way. When you are caught up in the politics of the day or watching the news. When you are arguing with a loved one. When there is an unexpected and unwanted change in your finances, health, relationship, career, home, etc. When people are just not being nice to you today. The external circumstance is the mirror. The fear, belief, thought, emotion, action, or reaction you respond with is your reflection in it. Your reflection is your life. There is nothing else.

We have discussed how success is about the quality of the journey and that the only time we are truly alive is in this moment. The quality of our lives is measured by the quality of the moments of our lives. When I choose to be angry, my life is filled with anger. When I choose to be depressed, my life is depressing. When I choose to hate others, then my life is filled with hate. When I choose to be afraid, then my life is filled with fear. If I was angry yesterday, that is what my day was about. If I was full of fear yesterday, that is what my day was about. If I have enough days like that this month, then that is how my month will be defined. If I have enough months like that, then that is how my year will be defined. If I have enough years and decades like that, then that is how my life will be defined.

When we change the meaning of our moments, we change the meaning of our lives. Our life is about this moment, and this moment is all we ever truly have. The key is, when we feel angry in this moment, we stop looking at the mirror, and look inside ourselves to find the part of us choosing to be angry. "When we are disturbed, for any reason, it is an opportunity to discover the part of us that is not thinking as we want it to, and to change that part of us."

How do you respond to the example day-to-day situations? There is no right or wrong way to respond, and everyone responds a bit differently. I used to respond in a much different way than I respond now. These situations were the source of much fear and many unwanted thoughts, emotions, and behaviors, but these situations were also the catalyst for much-needed change and growth. I found that the one thing all my unwanted responses had in common was my inability or refusal to accept things I cannot change. When I choose not to accept something as being exactly as it is supposed to be exactly at this moment, I choose to be disturbed in all types of hilarious and not-so-hilarious ways.

When we allow external circumstances to affect us in an unwanted way, we give these external circumstances control of our lives. We put our power in something that we have no control over. Every time we respond in unwanted ways, we strengthen that response, and we strengthen the whole

"The world is happening to me" or "I am a victim of my life" paradigm.

As we continue to use life's circumstances to uncover the things holding us back and the things that are decreasing the quality of our lives, our paradigm will shift. As the unwanted aspects of ourselves and our lives show up less and less, the opportunities to improve our lives will show up more and more. The events of our lives shift from happening to us, and begin to happen because of us.

The opportunities to increase the quality of our lives have always been there. I repeat: The opportunities to increase the quality of our lives have always been there. It's just that our awareness and focus have been elsewhere. We just haven't been ready for them yet. We have been busy either responding to life in unwanted ways, or busy dealing with the circumstances that our unwanted responses produced. This is not to say that our whole life is like this; I am sure there are good aspects of each one of our lives.

The whole moral of this part of the story is this: Increasing your awareness of when you are choosing to be disturbed is one of the most important skills you can develop. In doing so, you will forever change the way you view the world and all the events in it. Your world will change, because you have changed how you look at your world. Moving from "the world is happening to me" to "the world is happening because of me" is one of the biggest paradigm shifts you can ever make.

LIFE IS YOUR MIRROR – THE WORLD IS HAPPENING BECAUSE OF YOU

As you focus more on the opportunities in your life, you will see situations that used to trip you up in a different light. You will begin to see patterns of circumstances and outcomes in your life. You will see these unwanted circumstances only ended up that way because of how you responded to them. You will begin to see now that by responding differently to a similar set of circumstances, you can create a different outcome. You will realize that, whether you knew it or not, you were always the one creating your life.

Just to the degree you will accept this as fact and act as if it were true in your life, are you given the power to intentionally create the life of your dreams. Whether you believe it is true or not, you are correct. I want this to sink in. This is a world-changing understanding, like being blind and suddenly seeing.

You have been laying the groundwork for this paradigm shift through all the chapters and exercises in this entire book. You have been learning the mechanics of conscious creation:

- **Define exactly who you want to be and what you want.**
- **Imagine it in as much detail as you can as already being accomplished.**
- **Step out in faith.**

This is where life, as a mirror, will reveal to you your true nature and your true power. There is a difference between understanding something and knowing something. Understanding can be theoretical. You can grasp and understand a concept. The only way to know something, though, is by experiencing it. You have read multiple times in this book, "There is wisdom and strength of character that only comes through experience." As you become the person you wanted to become and live the life you planned on living, you will see that you, in the past, created this life. That your current situation is due to something you did or chose not to do. That creating preceded the creation. You will experience this as actually happening in your life. You created this moment. You will begin to "know" that your life is happening because of you, in a very literal sense. If it wasn't for your desire and/or your belief in this future moment, this future moment never would have happened. This reality only happened because you defined it, believed in it, and walked toward it. More important than any of that; you became the caliber of person that can make these commands of life.

LIFE IS YOUR MIRROR – LIFE IS GIVING YOU WHAT YOU ARE
The essence of conscious creation is this simple fact. Life does not give us what we want; it gives us what we are. I can design a life in great detail, want it and desire it, believe it will come true, yet if my level of being is not up to the level of the desired life, then that life will never happen for me. What happens and is quickened by taking that first step in faith, is that we become the person we need to become along the way. It is all about the person we become along the way. Anything we do to increase ourselves increases our lives. That is why this book has been so heavy on exercises and skills that will help you strengthen your character and increase your level of being. This book is about helping you become more.

You have learned much and experienced much. I hope you have gotten a glimpse of what you are capable of. A glimpse of your true potential. We all come into this moment with a whole lifetime of evidence telling us something altogether different. Seemingly, everywhere we look, there is lack and strife and injustice. Seemingly, everywhere we look, there are threats to our instincts of survival. A lifetime of "proof" can take a long time to disprove. What you have embarked upon is a journey of forgetting. By forgetting the beliefs that limit us, we remember who and what we truly are.

The more you experience and know that you create your life, the stronger and wiser you will become. You will see how some coincidences are not coincidences at all. Your awareness of guidance and inspiration will increase at a rapid rate. You will develop "spiritual subtitles," as I like to call them. This is where the surface level of an event or communication triggers a deeper meaning within you, which is usually totally out of context with the surface level event or communication. This is where more and more, the mirror of your life acts like a parable, its meaning evolving as you evolve. You will see patterns emerge in your life and anticipate things happening in your life. You might not know how you will get where you are going, you just know that you will, and you begin to "feel" that the steps you need to take are already there; you just haven't seen them yet. You will feel as if your conscious mind and ego are but a pen in the hand of a much greater part of you. This part of you is the true author of your life.

Your life develops a certain magical quality to it. Everything seems to go your way. You always get a good parking spot. You always get a good table with a good view. Situations that could have become a problem ended up in the best way. The people in your life become your mirror as well. Everyone you meet is super nice to you. You always see the best version of whoever you come into contact with. It seems like the character traits you personify somehow bring to the surface the same quality in the people you meet. You enrich and bless the lives of all those you encounter. They will all benefit from this journey you have begun. They recognize the change in you, and want to know what you are doing, so they can increase the quality of their life as well. The world will become a much more beautiful place because you have begun this journey.

The more you realize that life results directly from who you are, the better a person you will become. There will be this spiritual feedback loop happening where you put out positive energy and intention, and get back positive energy and results, which makes you want to put out even more positive energy and positive intentions, which brings back even more positive energy and results, and on and on and on. This feedback loop will allow you to expand your belief and experience of what you are capable of. Your whole being will evolve in every conceivable way. You will have changed. You will have become different. You will have become more.

I am honored to share these ideas with you and to be a part of your life. You reading this book is the realization of my dream. It is the direct result of me practicing the principles within this book. I hope you have found something that will allow you to experience more of whatever you want in your life. That was the goal that writing this book has helped me achieve. I wanted to help others to experience this great gift I have been given.

Your life will never be perfect. That is the good news. It will always continue to get better, though, if you will work for it. The world is not what we think it is. I love you with all that I am.

APPENDIX A

VISUALIZATION ENHANCEMENT EXERCISES

Throughout this book, you will be using visualization techniques in a variety of ways. Visualization doesn't come naturally to everyone, but anyone can learn to do it. When I started visualizing, I wasn't very proficient with it. I learned by practicing the techniques I am about to share with you. In this appendix, I will walk you through a couple of exercises as well as give you a few tips on how to improve your ability to visualize.

When we talk about enhancing the qualities of visualization, we refer to those qualities as modalities and submodalities. The three primary modalities, or how we access and create reality in our mind, are visual, auditory, and kinesthetic. Visual is what we see. Auditory is what we hear or say to ourselves. Kinesthetic is both the feeling of our physical sensations and our emotional feelings. Two others that we will not focus on that might aid you are gustatory, what we taste, and olfactory, what we smell. Modalities are primarily concerned with the content of the memory or imagined experience. The who, what, when, and where of the experience.

Submodalities are how we structure our experiences in our minds. So instead of what we see, hear, or feel, submodalities define how we see, hear, and feel. Below is a list of some common submodalities. This will show you what submodalities are.

- **Visual-** Location of the image in your field of vision, size of image, is it framed like a TV or panoramic, black and white or in color, moving or still, associated (seeing through your eyes) or dissociated (seeing as if a neutral observer)
- **Auditory-** Volume, Speed, Location, Tonality
- **Kinesthetic-** Location of feeling, shape, movement, pressure, color, spin, density, weight

Now that we have that brief description out of the way, let's walk through a few exercises that will help you develop your ability to recall memories as well as create images in your mind.

EXERCISE: MODALITY WARM-UP

First, just experience these modalities one at a time. Evaluate on your own which one of these you feel strongest in. Knowing this will help you to create a strong context in which to build your imagined environments. Record these instructions and play them back to yourself.

Visual: Eyes open or eyes closed. Whatever works best for you. Bring up these images in your mind.

- The entry into your local supermarket.

- The last TV you owned.
- A park you have been to.

Now imagine the following.

- An entry door to a store you have never been to.
- A TV much bigger or smaller than your TV.
- A park you have never been to.

Some people have no problem creating images in their minds. I had to learn to find a context image from my memories first, a template, if you will, then, build upon the template. For example, if I imagined a purple spotted elephant, I would begin with a memory of an elephant and then imagine it's purple and then add the spots. A technique that helps me pull up an image from memory is simply telling my mind out loud, "Show me an image of an elephant. Show me an image of a truck. Show me an image of a house." It doesn't matter what it is. As you will hear often, it's all about repetition, repetition, repetition. If you have a hard time bringing up images, you need only to practice.

Auditory: Hear these sounds.

- A horn.
- Music.
- The sound of someone's voice.
- The wind blowing through the trees.
- The ocean.
- The sound of you talking to yourself.

Sounds can be very subtle. I find again that context allows me to access these a little better. To hear a horn, I might remember myself in traffic first. To hear music, I might remember a concert I went to or putting some earbuds in. To hear the wind in the trees, I might remember a forest or grove or park I have been to.

Kinesthetic: Feel these sensations.

- Feel your left foot on the floor. Now feel your right foot on the floor. Now feel both on the floor.
- Feel hot air coming out of the oven. Feel cold air coming out of the freezer.
- Feel your back against a chair. Feel the clothes on your body. Feel your nose on your face.
- Remember feeling enthusiastic.
- Remember feeling anxious.
- Remember feeling peaceful.

Again, context helps. Remember the situation you were in, then drill down on the individual sensations or emotions. The examples given for all three modalities were completely arbitrary. I just wanted you to get an idea of how to experience the building blocks of reality.

EXERCISE: SUBMODALITY WARM-UP

Bring to mind a memory that is very easy for you to remember and one with a clear image associated with it. Record these instructions and play them back to yourself.

Visual Submodalities

- If you had to reach out with your hand and touch the image, where would it be located?
- How big is the image? Larger than life, life-size, or smaller than life?
- Are you seeing this memory through your own eyes, or are you seeing yourself in this scene as if you were a neutral observer?
- Is it color or black and white?
- Is there movement or is it still?
- Is it framed or panoramic?

Auditory Submodalities

- What sounds do you hear?
- What direction are the sounds coming from?
- Are the sounds loud or soft?
- Are they high or low pitched?
- What is the tempo like? Is it fast or slow?
- Are you saying anything to yourself? If so, from what direction, what volume, what pitch, what tempo, etc.?

Kinesthetic Submodalities

- Are there any sensations in your body?
- Are you experiencing any emotions?
- Where in your body do you feel that sensation or emotion?

- What is the size of it?
- Is it moving?
- Is it dense or sparse?
- Is it heavy or light?
- Are there any other words you can think of to describe this sensation or emotion?

EXERCISE: ENVIRONMENT CREATION

Now things get really fun. You will use variations of this exercise throughout this book, and hopefully for the rest of your life. What you will do now is construct an environment in your mind, and every time you do this exercise you will come back to the same environment and continue to add detail to it. As you have done before, record the following instructions and play them back to yourself. Allow 10-15 seconds between instructions to allow yourself sufficient time to follow the instructions.

Have someone read this to you or record it and play it back to yourself. Don't worry if you cannot do something that is instructed. You will get better at this. Just do your best and move on to the next instruction.

Think of a park-like setting or grassy area you have been to before. Imagine the grass in that setting. Imagine the color of the grass. Imagine the length of the grass. Imagine the feel of the grass as you walk on it or reach down and touch it. Imagine the smell of the grass. Imagine how much grass there is and how far it goes. Imagine any sounds that are present.

Imagine a tree in that setting. Imagine how far it is from you. Imagine the leaves, branches, and the trunk of it. Imagine the color of the leaves. Imagine the color of the trunk. Imagine any sounds coming from it. Imagine the texture of the trunk.

Imagine walking up to the tree and touching it. Imagine what your hand and fingers feel like touching it. Imagine leaning up against the tree and what your body feels like against the tree.

Imagine the sky. Imagine the lightness or darkness. Imagine if it is clear or if there are clouds. Imagine the color of it. Imagine the size of it and where it begins and where it ends. Feel the air touching your skin. Imagine the temperature of the air or the movement of the wind. Imagine any sounds that you are hearing.

Imagine any buildings in this setting. Imagine the shape and color of those buildings. Imagine walking up to those buildings and touching them with your hand. Imagine how your hand feels on the building.

Imagine a water feature. Imagine the size of it. Imagine the shape of it. Imagine any movement in it. Imagine walking up to it and putting your feet in it or touching it with your hand. Imagine how you experience the wetness of the water. Imagine the temperature of the water. Imagine seeing your reflection in the water. Imagine any sounds the water is making.

Imagine any other people that are present. Imagine family and friends. Imagine strangers and their families. Imagine any pets or animals that might be present. Imagine their voices. Imagine their faces as they are talking to you. Imagine hugging one of them and how that feels on your body. Imagine any other sounds the people or animals in this setting might be making.

Imagine what you are feeling in this setting. Imagine any emotions that are present. Imagine how you feel those emotions in your body. Imagine how you feel physically. Imagine touching your arm and how your hand feels touching your arm. Imagine your posture. Imagine your breathing.

VISUALIZATION ENHANCEMENT EXERCISES

Imagine closing your eyes and keeping them closed in this setting. Imagine remembering any details you can about this setting. Imagine stretching out your consciousness and "feeling" or "knowing" where everything was located.

Imagine that you are now viewing yourself in this scene as if you were a neutral observer. Imagine the scene you have created from this different perspective. Imagine yourself as if you were a bird flying by. Imagine the scene from this perspective.

Optional: Imagine that you are in this setting which is a tiny speck on the surface of the earth, the earth in space that is spinning around its axis at 1000 miles per hour, that is traveling around the sun at 67,000 miles per hour, that is spinning around the center of the galaxy at 490,000 miles per hour, that is traveling away from the center of the universe at 1.3 million miles per hour.

No doubt there is plenty in there that you weren't able to do yet. Just do the best you can. It doesn't need to be a park. It can be any setting you want. Mine is my dream home in the mountains. The key is to come back to this scene daily for at least five minutes and continue to add details. These details will be what you see, what you hear, what you feel, how you feel, what you taste, and what you smell. Run yourself through these questions again if you like. Adding people is very powerful. This allows you to see yourself in this setting from their vantage points.

Log on to **yourpowertochange.com** and create a login. This will give you access to the "Members Only" section, allowing you to print off Your Power to Change worksheets.

www.ingramcontent.com/pod-product-compliance
Lightning Source LLC
Chambersburg PA
CBHW072144100526
44589CB00015B/2075